AUTHOR

Eduardo Manuel Gil Martínez (25 June 1970) is a historian and has been passionate about Spanish history for several years, mainly about the Second World War and the age of the Reconquista. Author of numerous texts on the Second World War for Spanish and Italian magazines such as 'Revista Española de Historia Militar', AMARTE, 'Ritterkreuz' or 'The Axis Forces in the Second World War 1939-1945'. In addition to the title we publish, he is also the author of: "Sevilla Reina y Mora. Historia del reino independiente sevillano. Siglo XI', 'Breslau 1945. El último bastión del Reich', 'The Spaniards in the SS and the Wehrmacht. 1944-45. The Ezquerra unit in the Battle of Berlin ",' The Bulgarian Air Force in World War II. The forgotten ally of Germany', 'Romanian Armoured Forces in the Second World War', 'Hungarian Armoured Forces in the Second World War', 'Spanish Air Force in the Second World War', 'Hispano Aviación Ha-1112' (about the last Messerschmitt 109 ever built in Spain) and other texts for important publishers such as Almena, Kagero, Schiffer and Pen & Sword.

For the photos, we would like to thank:
FORTEPAN: Berkó Pál, Tarbay Julia, Doboczi Zsolt, Kókány Jenő, Ludovika, Varga Csaba dr., Csorba Dániel, Lissák Tivadar, Nagy Gyula, Konok Tamas Id, Miklós Lajos, Gadoros Lajos, Lakatos Maria, Marics Zoltán, Nagypal Geza, Vargha Zsuzsa, Lázár György, Mihalyi Balazs, Klenner Aladar, Scrutatore Ferenc, Kramer Istvan Dr, Ungvary Krisztian, Károly Németh, Péter Mujzer.

PUBLISHING'S NOTES

None of unpublished images or text of our book may be reproduced in any format without the expressed written permission of Luca Cristini Editore (already Soldiershop.com) when not indicate as marked with license creative commons 3.0 or 4.0. Luca Cristini Editore has made every reasonable effort to locate, contact and acknowledge rights holders and to correctly apply terms and conditions to Content.
Every effort has been made to trace the copyright of all the photographs. If there are unintentional omissions, please contact the publisher in writing at: info@soldiershop.com, who will correct all subsequent editions.
Our trademark: Luca Cristini Editore©, and the names of our series & brand: Soldiershop, Witness to war, Museum book, Bookmoon, Soldiers&Weapons, Battlefield, War in colour, Historical Biographies, Darwin's view, Fabula, Altrastoria, Italia Storica Ebook, Witness To History, Soldiers, Weapons & Uniforms, Storia etc. are herein © by Luca Cristini Editore.

LICENSES COMMONS

This book may utilize part of material marked with license creative commons 3.0 or 4.0 (CC BY 4.0), (CC BY-ND 4.0), (CC BY-SA 4.0) or (CC0 1.0). We give appropriate attribution credit and indicate if change were made in the acknowledgments field. Our WTW books series utilize only fonts licensed under the SIL Open Font License or other free use license.

For a complete list of Soldiershop titles please contact Luca Cristini Editore on our website: www.soldiershop.com or www.cristinieditore.com. E-mail: info@soldiershop.com

Title: **HUNGARIAN ARMOURED UNITS DURING THE SECOND WORLD WAR - VOL. 2: 1944 - 1945**
Code.: **WTW-048 EN** by Eduardo Manuel Gil Martínez
ISBN code: 9791255890362 first edition October 2023
Size: 177,8x254mm. Cover & Art Design: Luca S. Cristini

WITNESS TO WAR (SOLDIERSHOP) is a mark of Luca Cristini Editore, via Orio, 33/D - 24050 Zanica (BG) ITALY.

WITNESS TO WAR

HUNGARIAN ARMOURED UNITS DURING THE SECOND WORLD WAR

VOL. 2: 1944 - 1945

PHOTOS & IMAGES FROM WORLD WARTIME ARCHIVES

EDUARDO MANUEL GIL MARTÍNEZ

BOOKS TO COLLECT

CONTENTS

1944: BETWEEN A ROCK AND A HARD PLACE..5
CONSIDERATIONS ON THE FIGHTING IN THE YEAR 1944.....................5
THE FIGHT FOR GALICIA...6
MAGYARS IN POLAND..26
FIGHTING IN THE CARPATHIANS AND TRANSYLVANIA.......................29
THE BATTLE OF TORDA...37
BATTLES FOR SOUTHERN HUNGARY: ARAD, TISZA, SZENTES............44
DEBRECEN, THE GATEWAY TO BUDAPEST..50
THE SIEGE OF BUDAPEST..57

1945: THE FINAL BATTLES..69
THE SWAN SONG OF THE HUNGARIAN ARMOURED FORCES............69
BUDAPEST RESCUE ATTEMPT...73
THE LAKE BALATON OFFENSIVE...75
THE FINAL FIGHTS..77

ANNEXES
ANNEX 1: ARMOURED VEHICLES OF THE HUNGARIAN ARMY...........79
ANNEX 2: HUNGARIAN ARMOURED TRAINS..96
ANNEX 3: NUMBER OF ARMOURED VEHICLES DEPLOYED BY THE HUNGARIANS...97

BIBLIOGRAPHY..98

1944: BETWEEN A ROCK AND A HARD PLACE

CONSIDERATIONS ON THE FIGHTING IN THE YEAR 1944

The second half of 1944 turned into hell for Hungary. The initial offensive from the north-east was joined by one from the south-south-east and finally from the south-west. Countless battles took place all over Hungary many times simultaneously. Faced with this fact, we have decided to divide most of the actions of the Hungarian armoured forces into several campaigns or battles, which in some cases coincide in time.

To facilitate the understanding of the Soviet advance through Hungarian lands, we can roughly classify the events chronologically as follows:

- Fighting in the Carpathians (from the east and northeast of the country).
- Fighting in occupied Transylvania (south of the country): Torda.
- Fighting in southern Hungary: in Arad, along the Tisza River, Szeged and Szentes.
- Fighting in the hinterland of eastern Hungary: Debrecén.
- Siege of Budapest.
- Attempt to liberate Budapest.
- Fighting in western Hungary: Sóred, Lake Balaton.
- Last fighting in the north-west of the country and in Slovakia.

As a special mention, we will include the activities of the 1st Cavalry Division in the Polish lands, which played an exemplary role in subsequent fighting in retreat.

When the battle for Hungary began, the Soviet High Command arranged the following routes for its troops:

- 4th Ukrainian Front (formed on 5 August 1944): with the task of advancing towards the mountain passes of the north-eastern Carpathians and then heading towards Ungvár (Uzhorod) and Munkács (Mukachevo), thus capturing what today corresponds to Ukrainian Transcarpathia.
- 2nd Ukrainian Front: located further south than the previous one, was ordered to advance towards Debrecen, Kolozsvár (Cluj), Szeged and then cross the Tisza (Tisa) river.
- 3rd Ukrainian Front: although initially deployed in the Balkans, after completing its actions in Yugoslavia, it was directed northwards, also participating in actions in Budapest and western Hungary.

Another event to be taken into account in the second half of 1944 was the Slovak uprising in late August, which, although initially quelled in the period between 28 August and 28 October, caused serious disruptions in the transit of German supplies to the south and the deployment of German troops in Slovakia instead of on the Hungarian front. Another important consequence of the uprising was the final loss of the Dukla Pass to the Soviets on 6 October, after more than a month of fighting to capture it, leaving the northern gateway to Hungary in enemy hands.

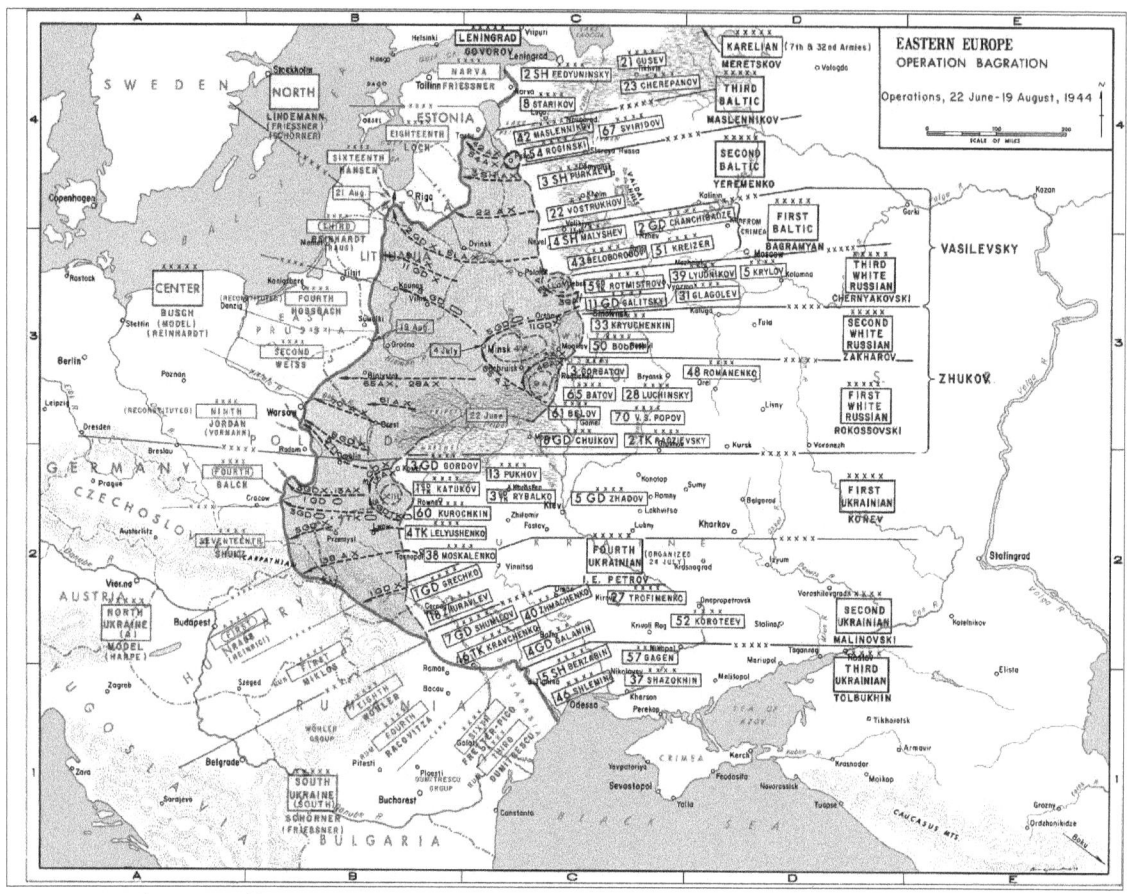

▲ Operation 'Bagration' between 22 June and 19 August 1944. Public domain.

THE FIGHT FOR GALICIA

After the Stalingrad disaster of February 1943, the demoralised Hungarians reconsidered the feasibility of their alliance with the Germans. The absence of strict control over Hungarian troops and their movements did not please the German High Command. Thus, in February 1944, they decided to change their attitude towards the Hungarians, who continued to ask the Germans for material and other aid. They would help the Hungarians, but the German troops would mix with the Magyars, reinforcing and controlling them and preventing any attempt at a Hungarian defection from the Axis. All this finally led the Germans to occupy 'allied' Hungary on 19 March 1944 in the so-called 'Operation Margarethe'. German troops from neighbouring Austria and also Croatia entered Hungary peacefully to deploy on Hungarian territory, but without going beyond the river Tisza, where the Hungarian 1st Army was deployed at the time, to avoid clashes. On the political front, meanwhile, Hitler decided to keep Regent Horthy in office, but forced him to make profound changes in both his government and the military high command, replacing many of its members with pro-German ones. General Lakatos, who had commanded the Hungarian occupation force in the USSR (and whom the Germans did not trust), was promoted to commander of the 1st Army. However, General János Vörös, who was the pro-German chief of staff, replaced him with another closer to the Germans: Beregfy. However, he was one of the least popular

▲ A Hungarian Fieseler Fi-156 light aircraft in support of ground troops.

Hungarian generals due to his limited leadership ability. Only after the German 'occupation' was Hungary finally able to fully mobilise its troops, with the 1st, 2nd and 3rd Armies in service; the 1st and 2nd Armoured Divisions were subordinate to them.

It is worth mentioning at this point that after the experiences on Soviet soil, Honved underwent several modifications in 1943 to make it more effective given the circumstances of the front closer and closer to Hungary. The first attempt was called the Szabolcs I plan, which was updated in early 1944 with the Szabolcs II plan. Some of the changes included assigning heavier artillery to infantry units and obtaining more 75 mm PaK40 anti-tank guns from the Germans. It was also decided that, for greater effectiveness, the Hungarian infantry should have its own assault tank support (each infantry division was to have an assault tank battalion).

With the same idea in mind, the reorganisation of the troops became more evident already in January 1944. Due to the approach of the Soviets, the entire Magyar Army was mobilised on 6 January and the 1st Army immediately blocked the mountain passes of the Carpathians (with the 16th and 24th Infantry Divisions and the 1st and 2nd Mountain Brigades). In February 1944, of the 45,000 men of the Magyar Army, 36,000 were deployed in the Hungarian hinterland.

Thus, on 1 April, the 7th, 10th, 13th, 16th, 20th, 24th and 25th Assault Wagon Battalions (the 1st was created in September-October 1943) were created from the 2nd to 8th Training Groups created in 1943, and the vehicles that were to equip them were, unfortunately, almost all assigned to the 1st Assault Wagon Battalion, due to the low production speed of the Zrínyi. Unfortunately, almost all of the vehicles that were to equip them were assigned to the 1st Assault Tank Battalion, due to the low production speed of the Zrínyi.

Due to the rapid Soviet advance already encamped in the westernmost parts of the Ukraine, in the spring of 1944 the Hungarian 1st Army was mobilised and positioned in the prepared defences in the Carpathians (started in the autumn of 1940 to take advantage of the natural defence offered by the Carpathians). But the Germans did not agree with this deployment so far behind the front line and ordered the Hungarians to move from the Carpathians to the Galician region. The mission of the Hungarian forces was to stabilise the situation between the German Ukrainian-North and Ukrainian-South army groups along the Kolomea-Ottyina-Stanislavov line. It should be remembered that the easternmost part of Ukraine and the south-easternmost part of Poland correspond to the historical region of Galicia (also known as Galicia), the most important city of which is Lvov (in English Lviv), and which was to become one of the targets of the Soviet army's numerous 'rides' to drive the invaders out of their country.

The Hungarian 1st Army consisted of three light infantry divisions (each with two regiments), three infantry divisions (each with three regiments), two mountain fighter brigades and, most importantly, the 2nd Armoured Division and the 1st Tank Battalion. The integration of Hungarian troops into the German machine is clearly visible by the inclusion of the 1st Hungarian Army in Field Marshal von Manstein's Army Group South.

▲ A Hungarian armoured train on Soviet territory. Its presence brought mobile firepower to the Hungarian troops.

The 2nd Armoured Division was mobilised on 13 March and was the most powerful unit of the entire Hungarian Army and, of course, of the 1st Army to which it belonged. The divisional artillery was also reinforced by the 1st Motorised Medium Howitzer Battalion (equipped with 150 mm 31M howitzers). One thing that characterised the 2nd Armoured Division was that all its equipment was of Hungarian origin, so its most powerful tanks were the 40M and 41M Turán, accompanied by the 40M Nimród, 39M Csaba and 38M Toldi. Due to the haste with which they were to be sent to the front and also due to the idiosyncrasies of the Hungarian industry, the units were not 100 per cent completed before being sent to the front. The equipment of the 2nd Armoured Division included 40 mm anti-tank guns (completely unsuitable for fighting Soviet tanks such as the KV-1 and T-34).

The 2nd Armoured Division had 120 Turán medium tanks, 55 Turán heavy tanks, 84 Toldi light tanks (47 of which were armed with 40 mm guns), 42 Nimród anti-aircraft tanks and 14 Csaba tanks. The Division also had a small fleet of 80 motorbikes and 160 trucks and cars. Ammunition was also in short supply, with approximately 30,000 40 mm shells for the Turan and 12,000 75 mm shells for the Turan. The Tank Regiment and its subordinate maintenance units had no spare parts or anything else to keep the tanks in proper working condition. Virtually every minor technical or operational problem rendered the tank useless for combat without the possibility of rapid repair.

▲ A Hungarian Fw-190 F8 in support of Hungarian troops.

▲ Two Turan I in a range exercise. Poorly armed and poorly armoured, they were no match for their Soviet counterparts.

For example, the 3rd Tank Regiment had 18 medium Turán, 14 heavy Turán, 1 Toldi and 2 Nimród. When the Division was transported to the front, this Tank Regiment had only 2 battalions, 3/I and 3/II. The 3rd battalion (3/III) remained in Hungary waiting to receive its tanks, before joining the rest of the unit at the front in July 1944.

The Soviets, in their continued pressure against the defensive line von Manstein held in Galicia, finally succeeded in breaking through it, causing a gap of more than 150 kilometres, practically the distance to the 1st Armoured Army of the German 8th Army, held only by the infantrymen of the Hungarian 7th Corps of the Hungarian 2nd Army. Von Manstein's German High Command decided that it would be his compatriots of the 1st Army who would fill the gap together with some German support units, so that a counter-attack could be launched on 7 April. Between 5 and 11 April 1944, the Hungarian 2nd Armoured Division, commanded by Colonel Osztovics, reached the assembly area at Stryj. From there they had to travel alone 250-300 kilometres to reach the front line, moving over muddy terrain with bad roads, covered in snow and virtually no rest. Once at the front, the deployment of the troops, who had to cover a sector of around 60-70 kilometres, meant that the various units of the Division were relatively separated from each other. To this end, the Division was divided into two combat groups, the stronger of which was under the command of Colonel Bercsényi (then commander of the 3rd Tank Regiment) and a second, less powerful group under the command of Colonel Sándor (then commander of the 3rd Motorized Rifle Regiment).

They did not have to wait long to make contact with the enemy, on 13 April in Lahowcze. Two Csaba, a Botond truck and a car were lost in this clash, as well as one dead and three wounded.

▲ A Turan crossing a bridge. The final model of this armoured vehicle was the Turan III, equipped with side and hull skirts and turret skirts. Another improvement of the 43M Turán III was the modification of the turret to accommodate a long 75 mm piece (the Hungarian copy of the powerful German 7.5 cm Pak 40, which in Hungary was called the 43 M L/55 75 mm) and thicker armour.

Another unit assigned to the Hungarian 1st Army was the 1st Assault Tank Battalion under the command of Captain Barankay (a veteran of the 1942 campaigns), whose main equipment was the brand new Hungarian-made Zrínyi assault howitzer. The Battalion's 2nd and 3rd Batteries left for the front on 12 April, arriving on the 16th of the same month. The Battalion Commander's involvement was such that, soon after arriving at the front, Barankay contacted a German tank assault unit operating nearby, the 301st Tank Assault Brigade (Sturmgeschütz). After obtaining permission, he was able to follow them on foot with some of his subordinates to observe and learn the tactics of the German tanks during the clashes with the Soviets.

Barankay was a military man bordering on fanaticism. This is shown by the fact that he sold his flat before joining his unit to march to the front, because he 'no longer needed it'. He also paid for a grave for his death in combat, among the first two soldiers of his Battalion to perish in service.

After many delays, the long-awaited first mission of the 2nd Armoured Division took place between 17 and 19 April, together with other Hungarian and German troops. The units that participated in the Axis attack were the Hungarian 6th Army Corps, the Hungarian 7th Army Corps (supported by a German Anti-Tank Battalion and an Assault Tank Battalion) and the German 11th Army Corps, where among other units the Hungarian 2nd Armoured Division operated. In addition to the ground troops, the attack also received the necessary air support.

The 2nd Armoured Division launched an attack from Solotwina towards Nadvorna, Delatyn and Kolomea, capturing the first two locations on 18 April after heavy fighting and establishing two bridgeheads on the banks of the Bistrica River. Taking stock, at that time it had only 17 75mm Turans (41M Turan), 31 40mm Turans (40M Turan) and some Toldi.

The bulk of the Hungarian attack was led by Colonel Bercsényi's battle group, with the Hungarians receiving support from German armoured units (15 Marder of the 615th Tank Hunter Battalion, 7 Pz IV and between 7 and 9 Tiger of the 503rd Panzer Battalion). On 17 April, the Turans engaged Soviet armoured vehicles for the first time, and although it was a mirage, they came out victorious, destroying two T-34s in exchange for the loss of two Turans north of Nadvorna. On 21 April, 3/I Battalion attacked two half-buried T-34s at Slobodca Lesna; six Turans were destroyed and killed. A total of four T-34s and one T-60

▲ A Turán tank crosses a military bridge. This armoured tank was not enough to compete on an equal footing with the Soviets, so the Hungarian armament industry tried to solve the problem with the Turán III. This new tank would have been a major step forward in increasing Hungarian armoured power, but it was still behind the modern tanks used by the Soviets in combat.

were destroyed and two German Marders were also lost. On the same day, 21 April, the 2nd Battery of the 1st Tank Assault Battalion made its debut on the front line in support of the 16th Hungarian Infantry Division at Bohorodchany. Despite the difficulty of the fighting, several American-made M3 half-tracks were captured intact after a Hungarian surprise attack from the flank. Soviet resistance was strenuous, so much so that, after being reinforced by an armoured brigade, they managed to lead a counter-attack on 22 April that stopped the Hungarian advance. The Hungarian infantrymen of the 16th Infantry Division were able to do little to counter the massive Soviet attack, but the intervention of the vehicles of the 1st Tank Battalion barely bridged the gap and then launched a counter-attack in which at least 17 T-34 tanks were put out of action. After regaining the lost ground, further counter-attacks by Zrinyi in the evening of the same day captured a village in the direction of Kolomea.

▲ The maximum armouring of the Turan was 50 mm at the front (up to 60 mm in more modern models). In the other parts of the wagon, the armour varied from 8 to 25 mm in the horizontal areas and from 25 to 40 mm in the vertical areas. On the Turan III, the front armour was to be 80 mm thick and 8 mm side skirts were to be fitted as standard on this tank.

These battles completely exposed the Turans, as a T-34 could fire at them with the possibility of destroying them from 1500-2000 metres away, while the Turans had to get as close as 600 metres if they had a 75-mm cannon or 400 metres if they had a 40-mm cannon. Moreover, the thickness of their armour was negligible for Soviet projectiles, although some Turans were equipped with side skirts, but these were insufficient due to their fragility when hit by enemy projectiles.

The attack by the Hungarian troops in collaboration with the Germans had been effective up to that point, as the Soviet units of the 4th Ukrainian Front and the 1st Guard Army were surprised. But once the Soviet lines were stabilised on 26 April, the Soviets began to take command of the attacks, forcing the Axis troops into defensive positions, which would remain stable until the end of July 1944. At least the Hungarian 1st Army had achieved its goal of establishing the link between the two German Army Groups.

Between 27 and 28 April, the 3rd Battery lost its commander, 1st Lieutenant Waczek. Due to the urgency of the situation, he had to take command of the battery himself during the ongoing fighting. At the end of the fighting, the command of the 3rd Battery passed to 1st Lieutenant Rátz.

The difficulty of holding the position in the face of the growing Soviet superiority in terms of men and tanks meant that on 30 April, the 2nd Battery was ordered to retreat in the direction of Stanislau.

The growing Soviet resistance meant that the second phase of the operation, centred on the capture of the town of Kolomea, was no longer the triumphant advance it had been up to that point. The terrain was very difficult, as the mud formed after the snowfall and the swollen rivers created numerous obstacles to the advance of the tracked and wheeled vehicles. In spite of this, the Soviets used the difficult terrain to their advantage, as the Hungarian

▲ The addition of side skirts to the Zrínyi II improved its survival during enemy engagements.

attack had to be slowed down and finally stopped on 3 May 1944 at Slovodka Lesna and Ocharnnyk, which meant that Kolomea would remain permanently in Soviet hands. In this advance, the 2nd DA suffered the loss of 24 tanks (9 Turán 75, 8 Turán 40, 4 Nimród and 2 Csaba). In addition, it is very unfortunate that at least 88 other tanks suffered various mechanical problems (6 of which could not be repaired and 7 others had to be left behind to be captured later by the Soviets). In total, 35 armoured vehicles were permanently lost and 75 had to be sent home for repair, due to the lack of proper maintenance of these tanks, as already mentioned. On the positive side, at least 48 Soviet armoured vehicles were destroyed, 27 of which belonged to the 3rd Hungarian Armoured Regiment of the 2nd Hungarian Armoured Division.

The losses of the 2nd Armoured Division amounted to 184 dead, 1153 wounded and 112 missing between 17 April and 13 May. The 3rd Motorised Rifle Regiment lost 1060 men and the Tank Regiment 384. These human and material losses rendered the 2nd Armoured Division completely useless for use at the front and it was withdrawn from the front line to join the 1st Hungarian Army Reserve on 12 May. General Model, commander of the North Ukrainian Army Group, praised the fighting spirit of the Hungarian armoured forces during the battles they fought.

It was clear that the Hungarian-built armoured vehicles were not up to the standard of the Soviet armoured forces; moreover, the level of maintenance was minimal, which, together with the virtual lack of spare parts, made the situation unfavourable for the Hungarians. For this reason, on 4 May, the German High Command agreed with the Hungarian government to partially re-equip the 2nd Armoured Division with German equipment. Thus, between 6 and 14 May, 12 PZ IV H, 10 Pz VI E Tiger and 10 StuG III G were delivered to Nadvorna. Battalion 3/I was equipped with German equipment, while Battalion 3/II was equipped with Hungarian Tigers. In order to prepare the new Hungarian Tiger crews, preliminary training under German soldiers was required for their use at Kolomyia, on the Prut River and temporary headquarters of Schwere Panzer-Abteilung 509. The Magyars were to receive the new Tiger tanks received from Schwere Panzer-Abteilung 509, but contrary to the orders received, the Germans gave them the most used tanks, including some battered tanks they had received in May from Schwere Panzer-Abteilung 503. This training took place between May and June 1944 in Nadvorna, which had already become the next Soviet target.

After the German re-equipping, the 3/I Battalion had four companies, the first with 11 Pz IV H, the second with six Tigers, the third with six Tigers and the fourth with nine StuG III. The companies with the powerful Tigers were commanded by 1st Lieutenant Ervin Tarczay and Captain János Vetress. The surplus vehicles left by the various companies were in turn handed over to the Division's 3rd/2nd Battalion. In addition to the 10 Tiger vehicles received, the Germans gave three more as a birthday present to Major General Hollósy-Kuthy, then Inspector of Hungarian Engineering. The Hungarians distributed them by sending two of them to the companies that already owned Tigers a and the remainder were kept to become part of the training unit for the new German equipment, as the Hungarians expected the new German equipment to arrive shortly. In this training unit commanded by Lieutenant Eszes, a Pz IV H and a StuG III were available in addition to the Tiger. However, no other German material was to be received any time soon.

▲ New Hungarian crew members give their full attention to German instructors in the turret of a Tiger.

After about a month of learning how to handle the new mounts, the last step for the complete conversion of the new Hungarian crews into German vehicles was their use in the firing line. Thus they were incorporated into the fighting of the German 24th Infantry Division. The tanks acted with their Hungarian crews in support of these troops. In this training provided by the Germans to the Hungarians, 3 T-34s and several Soviet anti-tank guns were destroyed by the Hungarians.

With the arrival of new Zrínyi from the factories, new tank battalions began to be reinforced; the 7th tank battalion was formed in Sümeg, the 10th in Szigetvár, the 13th in Csongrád, the 16th in Debrecen, the 20th in Eger, the 24th in Kassa and the 25th in Kolozsvár. However, as there was no Zrínyi to complete them all, Toldi and Turán continued to be used.

Around 19 May, the 3rd Battery of the 1st Assault Tank Battalion was sent south of the village of Pruth, where it would operate as an independent unit under XI Corps, which was part of the Hungarian 1st Army. The 3rd Battery was first engaged in combat on 20 May in the Peczenyczyn area (south-east of Ukrainian Kolomea).

In mid-June the 1st Battery of the 1st Assault Tank Battalion under the command of 1st Lieutenant Sandor finally arrived at the front from Hajmáskér with 10 Zrínyi, thus making it the first time that the entire 1st Assault Tank Battalion was at the front (10 vehicles per Battery and one additional command vehicle). The 3rd Battery under the command of Sub-Lieutenant Rátz made an attack on the Soviet positions on 9 July at Pechenizhyn, where a Zrínyi fell into a trench and was abandoned in enemy territory only to be recovered the next day under enemy fire by Sub-Lieutenant Rátz (for which he received the Iron Cross 2nd Class on 11 July 1944).

▲ Another picture of a Hungarian StuG III, in this case with side skirts. This vehicle of German origin gave a considerable boost to the effectiveness of the Hungarian armoured forces.

▲ Magyar soldiers posing on the back of a Pz IV H with side skirts.

At the end of June and during July, a group of Hungarian tank soldiers travelled to Magdeburg, Germany, to retrain in the use of tanks. However, the six weeks of training had to be shortened after Hitler's assassination attempt on 20 July 1944.
Sure enough, on 13 July the Soviet army launched an offensive towards Sandomierz and Lvov (Lviv), the former in south-eastern Poland and the latter in Galicia, causing a break in the front line held by Hungary. Marshal Koniev's 1st Ukrainian Front acted as a battering ram against the weak Axis defence lines, which consisted of Heeresgruppe Nordukraine comprising the 4th Panzer Army on the left flank, the 1st Panzer Army in the centre and the Hungarian 1st Army on the right flank. For this reason the 2nd Armoured Division was put on alert and deployed urgently to Stanislau on 23 July, while the rest of the Hungarian 1st Army sought shelter in the Carpathians where it would take up position in the incomplete fortifications of the 'Hunyadi' line.
During the Soviet offensive in July, the 1st Tank Battalion suffered heavy losses and the 1st and 2nd Batteries had to be used as rearguard units to slow the Soviet advance east of Ottynia. Captain Barankay was killed in an air raid on 13 July in the town of Targowica (still within its lines) while directing his vehicles towards Ottynia, leaving the unit under the command of Major Doory, who had arrived from Hungary at the end of July. Captain Barankay was buried with full honours in Stanislau. In August 1944, after his death, he was awarded the Officer's Gold Medal for exemplary leadership of his battalion during the fighting in the Galician campaign. József Barankay Rohamtüzér Osztály" (1st Assault Tank Battalion József Barankay) as a tribute to Barankay.

▲Ervin Tarczay poses on his Pz VI Tiger in this front view. With this vehicle he achieved many of his victories in various battles. June 1944.

In the massive Soviet attack, the 3rd Battalion could not hold it off and several Hungarian Tiger troops trying to reach the north of Stanislau were pushed back. This prompted the Hungarian 1st Army to finally order the withdrawal of these troops, ordering the Tiger troops to act as a rearguard for the retreat. This was precisely a mission for which the Tiger had a great capacity due to its great armour and better weaponry; in addition, the favourable conditions of the terrain through which their compatriots were retreating, with narrow mountain roads diminishing the superiority of material with which the Soviets could confront the Hungarians. In one such battle near Saturnia, Ervin Tarczay, the Hungarian armoured ace, in command of two Tiger tanks, managed to destroy 14 enemy armoured vehicles (mainly T-34s) on Hill 514 in half an hour without suffering any losses.

But after the Soviets, the Hungarians' main problem was also their modern German vehicles: the lack of petrol, spare parts and much-needed tractors to tow the damaged vehicles for repairs definitely hampered their ability to reorganise and become an offensive force again. Under these circumstances, they were forced to perform defensive tasks aimed at causing maximum attrition to the Soviets, whose material and human supplies seemed inexhaustible.

It should be noted that this withdrawal requested by the Hungarian Chief of Staff, Colonel General Vörös, was not initially authorised by the German High Command. The reason was the inability of the Hungarian troops to resist the Soviet assault on the deployed positions and, although this was an obvious fact, it did not occur until the new Soviet attack on 22 July. From then on, despite the attempt to proceed as orderly as possible, the infrastructure and rugged terrain were of little help.

From 24 to 29 July, the armoured units of the 2nd Armoured Division engaged in continuous fighting against the Soviets, fighting along the Czuczylow-Grabevjec-Horohodina-Saturnia-Rosulna-Kraszna-Rozniatow-Dolina route. This constant fighting caused the number of armoured vehicles in service to decrease drastically: 3/I Battalion lost seven Tiger tanks due to the wear and tear of the fighting, only three of which reached Hungarian territory. For its part, 3/III Battalion, which had been left in Hungary to complete its training, finally rejoined its comrades in July. On 22 July, this Battalion suffered its first losses in its baptism of fire and continued to suffer losses in subsequent battles, such as those of 24 July at Milanowie and 26 July at Dzwiniacz.

On the same 24 July, the 2nd Battery of the 1st Tank Battalion ambushed 3 T-34s in Winograd and managed to destroy them. This action, together with the one conducted on the same day on his own initiative by Lieutenant Buszek of the 2nd Battery, repulsed a Soviet rifle unit that had surrounded a Hungarian artillery battery. Three days later, the 1st Tank Battalion joined the 2nd Armoured Division to keep the escape route open for the retreating troops in the Lukwa Valley, in the direction of Rozniatow, Dolina and finally Wygoda. The only escape route was the aforementioned Lukwa Valley, which had been collapsed by the fleeing

▲ The training of the Hungarian crews on the new vehicles received from Germany was carried out by the Germans. Here you see a Pz VI in the foreground, a StuG III and a Pz IV H in the background.

troops pursued by the Soviets. The 1st Tank Battalion was ordered to keep the way open at all costs, eliminating any existing obstacles. The Battalion's Zrinyi also acted as improvised transport vehicles for the multitude of wounded trying to save their lives. In this combat, more than two thirds of the Zrinyi were lost.

The 1st and 2nd Batteries suffered heavy losses during this operation, but managed to reach the Hungarian border on 28 July, together with the staff of the 1st Tank Battalion, through the Toronya Pass in the north-eastern Carpathians. The 1st Tank Battalion settled in the village of Felsöveresmo, near Hust, where the Hungarian 1st Army staff had arrived shortly before after its retreat. The 1st Battalion remained in Felsöveresmo until the end of September 1944.

For its part, the 3rd Battery under the command of Rátz, having operated in areas less exposed to Soviet attacks and not having been involved in the bulk of the fighting, managed to return safely to Hungary through the Tatár Pass with its 10 Zrínyi. The support vehicles of the 3rd Battery managed to cross the Deatyn Bridge over the Pruth River, but the heavier vehicles had to cross the river a little further south. After arriving in Hungary, the battery was deployed in Korosme.

The tremendous attrition suffered by the 2nd Armoured Division led to the decision to withdraw it from the front line and reorganise at Huszt. On 9 August, the arsenal of the 2nd Armoured Division consisted of 14 Toldis, 40 Turán-40s, 14 Turán-75s, 1 Panzer III, 1 StuG III G and 9 Panzer IV H. Three Tigers had also survived the heavy fighting, but were damaged enough that it was decided to withdraw them for further repairs. Hungarian ace Tarczay was thus left without his fabulous mount, although he would soon return to command another tank of German origin, the Panther.

Due to the position of the Hungarian troops in the Carpathians and the difficulties this posed for the Soviet troops, there was a slight pause in the offensive. This pause served to replenish losses and improve reserves, so as to prepare thoroughly for the next attack, which would take them into the Magyar lands. In the meantime, the Hungarians took the opportunity to improve their positions on the 'Hunyadi' line as much as possible and to prepare for the imminent Soviet attack. Among these Hungarian moves was the replacement in August 1944 of the depleted 1st Tank Assault Battalion (with only a third of its initial combat strength) with the 10th Tank Assault Battalion that had been formed in Szigetvár at its positions in the Carpathians. To make the 10th Battalion combat-ready, Zrínyi were collected from all sides (from the other battalions in formation); the 3rd Battery of the 10th was also to be formed from the surviving Zrínyi of the 3rd Battery of the 1st Tank Battalion.

During the Soviet offensive in Galicia, the situation at the front was terrifying for the Hungarians. In spite of this, and thanks to their armoured forces, which were very limited in both quantity and quality, they managed to hold the escape route for the rest of the Axis troops, while preventing the Red Army from initially entering Hungarian territory.

The 7th Tank Battalion received 31 StuG IIIs from the Germans and was ready to leave for the front at the end of August, with only a few days to train with the new vehicles. The 7th Tank Battalion would then fight as part of the 3rd Army in Arad in September of the same year.

▲ In addition to the undeniable defensive advantage that the side skirts gave the Zrínyi II, there was also an increase in the vehicle's weight and thus a reduction in its ability to move. This vehicle was captured by the Soviets and is now on display in the museum in Kubinka.

▼ The remains of Captain Barankay of the 1st Tank Battalion lie in a Zrínyi II guarded by his honour guard.

▲ Two Nimród participate in an anti-aircraft fire drill in Galicia. Some infantrymen are seen relaxing and 'enjoying' the exercise.

▼ Close-up of Lieutenant Ervin Tarczay (left), the most famous ace of the Hungarian armoured forces in World War II.

▲ The fording of a river by a Turán II causes excitement among some Magyar engineer soldiers during a break in the fighting in Galicia in 1944.

▼ In this photo of Tarczay on his Tiger, we can see both the German emblem on the tank and its number, indicative of the 2nd Company of the 3rd Battalion of the 2nd Armoured Division. Picture taken in Galicia in June 1944.

▲ A column of Hungarian StuG IIIs advances into the combat zone. The 7th Tank Battalion received most, but not all, of these vehicles.

▼ Tarczay with his Pz VI Tiger. Hungary was the only one among Germany's allies to possess a few units of this brilliant German tank.

MAGYARS IN POLAND

One unit we have not mentioned is the 1st Cavalry Division, which was mobilised on 29 April 1944 (26th according to Bernád) and sent to the front. The Hungarian idea was to subordinate it to the 1st Army deployed in the Carpathians and place it on its left wing, but the Germans rejected this idea and the hussars were sent separately from the other Hungarian units, i.e. to the Pripet marshes (southern Belarus and north-western Ukraine). There they formed the reserve of the German 2nd Army under the name Hungarian Reserve Corps after arriving at Pinsk on 20 June and at Luninets on 21 June. However, this mission was only on paper, as they soon found themselves engaged in anti-partisan activities near the railway lines in the area and, after the start of 'Operation Bagration', became a frontline unit. In addition, the 1st Cavalry Division was divided into smaller divisions that operated separately from each other. For example, the 2nd Hussar Regiment fought the partisan troops in Luninniec.

This unit comprised the 1st Cavalry Tank Battalion, which had one heavy tank company, three medium tank companies and one command company. In total there were 25 38M Toldi, 54 40M Turan 40, 11 41M Turan 75. According to other sources, there were 65 medium, 11 heavy, 5 Toldi and three Pz 38. The 15th Cyclist Battalion of the 1st Cavalry Division also had a platoon with 4 40M Nimród.

The Soviet offensive overwhelmed the entire defensive line of Army Group Centre, forming a huge gap. The Hungarian cavalry troops had to move about 150 km to the east to stop the Soviets. By 30 June the city of Slutsk had fallen and the Hungarian Division had to retreat northwards.

▲ One of the Pz III M received by the Hungarians in September 1942 to try to overcome the immense losses suffered on the Don front.

After the first days at the front, on 2 July 1944, the 1st Cavalry Tank Battalion split into two battle groups:
- The 4th Heavy Tank Company was subordinate to Colonel Schell's battle group at Tinkovicze (this group included, in addition to the heavy tank company, one and a half regiments of hussars, two and a half artillery battalions, an anti-aircraft battery and an armoured vehicle platoon), which was also supported by a German destroyer company. This battle group had the task of replacing the German 4th Cavalry Division at the Tinkovicze bridgehead.
- The rest of the 1st Cavalry Tank Battalion and the 3rd Reconnaissance Battalion were held in reserve in Kletsk.

On 3 July, they reached the combat zone where they were faced with four Soviet armoured units far superior in men and equipment. The Schell Group launched an attack on 3 July from Tinkovicze, but it was repulsed by the Soviets, who took advantage of the situation to launch a counter-attack with their armoured units in Snolice and nearby areas. In this situation, the 75th Turan was the only one able to counter the enemy without suffering losses. However, the retreat meant that the Hungarian troops were surrounded at Kletsk, so they were ordered to break through the encirclement across the Cerpa River, using the 4th Heavy Tank Company commanded by Captain Reök and supported by the 4th Engineer Company (panzerfaust army) as a spearhead. From this position they moved in the direction of the Shchara River. The engagement took place on 4 July in Cerpa and several victories were achieved over the Russian tanks, at the cost of losing two Turans. Captain Reök lost an arm in the heavy fighting that finally allowed the Hungarians to escape the encirclement. Despite the immense difficulties and heavy losses, the escape from encirclement in the direc-

▲ Photograph showing a Toldi II with a pair of Toldi I's behind it. One can see the emblem that would be used by the Hungarian armoured forces from 1942 onwards.

tion of the Shchara River can be considered a success, in which the armoured forces, despite their modesty, did their duty.

On 6 July, the cavalry troops took up defensive positions in the Mishanka area, but were forced to retreat the next day when they were threatened with encirclement by the lightning advances of the Soviets on their flanks. After two weeks of fighting, the unit had lost almost all its horses and had to continue fighting on foot as infantry.

On 13 July, Russian troops penetrated between the positions of the 3rd Hungarian Hussar Regiment and the 102nd German Infantry Regiment. In this situation, the 15th Cyclist Battalion launched an attack from Duzuny and succeeded in repelling the Soviets after hand-to-hand combat.

The 1st Cavalry Division had to 'fill' a large gap in the German defence lines, which it did at first, despite the enemy's superiority. After leaving the Kletsk pocket and until 25 July, the 1st Cavalry Division found itself in a continuous fighting retreat in the direction of the Vistula River. Along the way, a large part of the Division's fleet was lost. In fact, the 1st Cavalry Tank Battalion lost all its tanks (84 in total) and the 3rd Reconnaissance Battalion had only 6 Csaba out of the original 23. Until 15 July, the losses of the various units ranged from 30 to 40 per cent of their strength.

From August 1944, the 1st Cavalry Division was reorganised and received some German equipment. Mainly anti-tank guns and anti-tank light weapons. Only the 2nd Cavalry remained fully mounted, while the 3rd and 4th had an infantry battalion and a battalion of mounted troops. The Division also received ten Hetzer tank destroyers as support (the first vehicles of this type received by the Magyars). The Division's commander, Major General Ibrányi, refused the Germans the possibility of being sent to fight the Polish forces maintaining the uprising in Warsaw, referring to the traditional friendship between Poles and Hungarians. During this cooling-off period, the unit was christened the 'Hussar Division' in recognition of its excellent performance in combat.

The cavalry division's operations in Poland ended in September 1944, so it was sent back to Hungary, where it would be reinforced with troops but would not receive any more armoured vehicles.

▲ Hungarian cavalry troops on reconnaissance mission.

FIGHTING IN THE CARPATHIANS AND TRANSYLVANIA

We had left the Soviets in the Galician countryside and were ready to begin the attack on the Hungarian Carpathians. Remember that the Carpathians form a mountain range that starts from the Danube at Bratislava, curves north-east towards the Tatra Mountains, turns south-west towards Transylvania and reaches the Danube again at Orsova and the so-called 'Iron Gate'.

During the retreat from Galicia, the 2nd Armoured Division covered the retreat of its compatriots by positioning itself in the area of the village of Dolina, holding it for two days against the advancing Soviet army. Fortunately, the Hungarian 1st Army had managed to re-enter Hungarian territory to take up position in the "Hunyadi" defensive line after neatly abandoning the "Prinz Eugen" line. It is interesting at this point to comment on the defensive lines that the Hungarian troops had constructed and rehabilitated from 1940 to 1944 throughout their geography to defend their borders in the event of an attack by one of their enemies, but concentrating on this occasion on the Carpathian front. The 'Hunyadi' line was not the only such line in the Carpathians, which were three in all, to which was added one located before the Carpathian foothills in Galicia (we refer to the aforementioned 'Prinz Eugen' line, the most exposed to the enemy, which ran from Kovel southwards and was located some ten kilometres from the front in May 1944).

The 'Hunyadi' line had been built by the construction troops of the 1st Army and consisted of multiple parapets and strongpoints constructed of earth and wood, surrounded by barbed wire and anti-tank obstacles that would have aided Hungarian defensive tactics. This line was not a true fortified defence line in the classical sense of the term, but 'straddled' various elevations of the north-eastern Carpathians just in front of the Hungarian border. Directly behind the Hungarian border was the 'St. László' line, which ran along the Hungarian border. László', which literally ran along Hungary's historical border (it had numerous trenches

▲ In case of luck, transfers of Hungarian troops to the USSR took place by rail.

and fortifications built during the First World War that made it all but impregnable and was supported by a number of high ground that protected the mountain passes of Tatár, Pantyr, Toronya, Verecke and Uzsok), while further back, taking advantage of the rugged terrain and punctuated by numerous interconnected strongpoints, was the more strongly prepared 'Árpád' line. This last defensive line, the 'Árpád', was established between the towns of Körömezö and Fenyvesvölgy, and provided cover for the roads that ran through the valleys behind the mountainous area; to provide more security in depth, a smaller defensive line was created about 5-10 kilometres behind the 'Árpád'. Since the Magyars had set up their own defensive lines, perhaps the most feasible option would have been to give up the frontal attack on the Hungarian lines and attack Hungary from the north through the Dukla River valley, on the border with Slovakia and just north of the Uzsok mountain pass; or from the south from Transylvania (although that area was covered by 'allied' Romania). The preparations and subsequent reorganisation of the Soviets were short-lived after the fighting of the previous months, as on 11 August the men of the Hungarian 1st Army began to be attacked. The Soviets were not Hungary's only concern, however, as on 25 August Romania changed sides after a coup d'état, then declared war on its Hungarian neighbour and finally joined the Soviets in an attack to conquer Transylvania (remember that this region was the subject of a dispute between Romanians and Hungarians). The last straw for the Romanian resistance to the Soviets was the battle for Iași and Chișinău in August 1944 (part of the Soviet offensive for Bessaravia and Moldavia between 20 and 29 August 1944), which left the 'gates' of Romania wide open to the Russian giant, as the German-Romanian defensive network was practically put out of action.

▲ One of the few photographs showing a Hetzer tank destroyer with Magyar insignia.

▲ An Ansaldo tank tries to ford a river in Transylvania.

▼ Cyclist troops in Transylvania, who played an important role in the taking of these lands.

▲ Hungarian armoured vehicles are greeted with applause on 13 September 1940 in Kézdivásárhely, a town in western Transylvania. In the foreground a Toldi I of the 2nd Reconnaissance Battalion with the tricolour insignia.

Having Romania as an enemy posed another problem, as the borders, especially in southern Transylvania, which until then had been held with second-class troops for guard duty (the original defence plan had been supported by the Romanian 'allies'), now became the front line, right through the 'back door' of the Magyar country. After Romania changed sides in September 1944, the Hungarian General Staff had to draw up a plan for the defence of western Transylvania. The idea was to form a defensive line in the Southern Carpathians, along the Romanian-Hungarian border, through a pre-emptive attack to prevent Russian and Romanian troops from advancing into Hungarian territory. To this end, a new 2nd Army was quickly organised and mobilised with two divisions, a reserve brigade and three divisions from the east, to which the 2nd Armoured Division was added. A weak 3rd Army was also formed with a regular division (20th Infantry), three reserve divisions (5th, 8th and 23rd Infantry) and other smaller units.

The combined Romanian-Soviet forces numbered 72 divisions, against which the Magyars could only deploy the aforementioned 2nd and 3rd Armies, which did not have enough men or modern weapons to face them with any guarantee of success.

At the same time, the Soviet forces facing the 'Hunyadi' line on the Carpathian front managed to break through the defensive network and penetrated into Hungarian territory on 27 September, where the defenders of the 'St. László' and 'Árpád' lines were waiting resolutely, ready to protect their homeland from the invader.

▲ A proud Hungarian soldier poses with a 40 mm Bofors 36M cannon.

Following the restructuring of the front after the new Soviet offensive, now supported by the Romanians, the Hungarian 2nd and 3rd Armies were subordinated to the German Southern Army Group, which had 30 divisions, 3500 artillery pieces, 300 tanks and about 500 aircraft. Opposing them was the mighty 2nd Ukrainian Front with 60 divisions, 10,000 artillery pieces, 7,800 tanks and 1,000 aircraft. The German Southern Army Group was divided into two operational battle groups, with the Hungarian 2nd Army and German 8th Army subordinated to the Wöhler Group, while the Hungarian 3rd Army and German 6th Army were integrated into the Fretter-Pico Group. In this way, the Hungarian units were to be completely controlled by the Germans to avoid any dissent.

The first attempt by the Romanians against the Hungarians on Hungarian territory took place on 25 August, when a Romanian infantry group crossed the border through the Keleman (Călimani) Mountains and clashed with the 23rd Battalion of the Border Guards.

Only a day later, Soviet infantry troops of the 7th Guards and armoured troops of the 23rd Armoured Corps crossed the border through the Úz and Csobányos valleys, as well as north of the Ciuc Mountains, effectively bringing the war onto Hungarian territory for the first time in the entire conflict.

The fighting in Transylvania involved the 10th Tank Assault Battalion, the 101st and 102nd Armoured Trains and the 2nd Armoured Division. The latter unit was commanded by Major General Zsedény, while the commander of the 3rd Tank Regiment was Colonel Balsay. In reality, the 2nd Armoured Division, after the continuous fighting in Galicia, was well below the desired level to fight. It had 14 Toldi, 40 40M Turán, 14 41M Turán 75, 21 40M Nimród and 12 39M Csaba. In addition, the 2nd Division was reinforced with one Pz III, 9 Pz IV H, 3 Tiger and one StuG III. On 4 September, due to the depletion of the Hungarian armoured arsenal, it was necessary to reach an agreement with the German Reich to send 20 Pz IVH and 5 Panther. The latter were assigned to the company of the 3rd Tank Battalion of 1st Lieutenant Taczay.

There are some doubts about the arrival of the Panthers, with sources claiming that 10-12 were received. What is certain is that there are no photographs showing Hungarian crews using them.

The 140 or so vehicles of the 2nd Armoured Division were transported by train from Esztergom and Hajmáskér to Szamosfalva, where they arrived on 5 September, the same date the Soviets took the town of Brasov. So in September 1944 the danger came from the south, as we can see, but in the northern part of Hungary the Soviets were trying to force the Dukla Pass (on the border with Slovakia) and in the west, as we have said, the "St. László" line had become the front line.

▲ 38M Toldi of the Light Cavalry Tank Company in Transylvania in 1940.

▲ Close-up of the narrow crew compartment of the Csaba tank.

▼ A column of 38M Botond in Transylvania.

▲ The majority of the Hungarian forces were not motorised, so in many cases the hypermobile option was chosen..

▼ Image of a Soviet armoured train put out of action. Some would later be reused.

▲ The Turán II, with its short 75 mm cannon, represented almost the pinnacle of Magyar tank production in the period in question.

THE BATTLE OF TORDA

At the end of August 1944, the Magyar high command decided to advance into the Southern Carpathians to reach the passes of Vöröstorony (Turnu Rosu) and Vulkán before the Soviets could conquer them, and then try to reach the Danube at the 'Iron Gates', where they would contact the retreating German troops from the Balkans. They were to face the Romanian 1st Army, which was still being reorganised, but would soon be joined by the reformed Romanian 4th Army. The Hungarian advance took place without any German support, as the Germans were focused on the process of withdrawal from Romania and fighting in other areas of the front.

The Hungarian 2nd Army under General Lajos Veress was mobilised together with the Hungarian IX and II Corps. The IX Corps concentrated on holding northern Transylvania, while the II Corps was responsible for the advance southwards. The II Corps had the 7th and 9th Replacement Divisions, but more troops would soon arrive from the north, including the 25th Infantry Division and the 2nd Armoured Division.

On 5 September 1944, the Hungarians launched an offensive against the outnumbered Romanian forces. The spearhead was the 2nd Armoured Division and within it the 2nd Tarczay Company, which had followed the Nagysármás-Mezõzáh-Mezõtóhát route to Marosluda on 5 September. From Marosluda, after crossing the Aranyos (Aries) river, they left at sunset on 5 September for Torda, where the Magyar attack began. In front of them, the Romanian 1st and 4th armies attempted to resist, but were initially overwhelmed. Armoured troops attacked the left flank to reach Dicsőszentmárton (Târnăveni) on 7 September, while in the centre the 9th Replacement Division took Marosújvár (Ocna Mureş) and Felvinc (Unirea), and the 7th Replacement Division was planted in front of Nagyenyed (Aiud). Among the units that took part in the offensive was the 25th Assault Tank Battalion (which had already participated in some fighting in Transylvania, but equipped only with 75 mm PaK 40 anti-tank guns). The commander of the 25th Tank Battalion, Vilmos Vértes, led it with great courage despite the lack of adequate equipment. On the first day of the battles for Torda, 5 September, the Battalion captured a large amount of equipment from the Romanians and many prisoners (including the commander-in-chief of the 20th Infantry Division, Major General Constantin Visarion). The need for more armoured troops meant that the 3rd Battery of the 1st Tank Battalion was transported by train to Nagyvárad (Oradea), from where it was positioned on the left flank of the Hungarian 3rd Army. The 3rd Battery, commanded by 1st Lieutenant Rátz, forced the Romanians to retreat from the village of Belenyes, where it lost its Zrínyi after being hit by a mine.

The beginning of the Magyar offensive was a success, reaching the town of Torda (Turda, today in Romania) ten days after its start and finally crossing the Maros (Mures) rivers.

Recovering from the initial blow, the Romanians sent the Mechanised Corps, 9th Infantry Division and 8th Motorised Cavalry Division against the Magyars around 8 September. Furthermore, the appearance of Soviet troops and General Rozin's Romanian Armoured Division finally stopped the Hungarians on 9 September in their attempt to reach the mountain passes in northern Transylvania. With the general retreat of the Hungarians, the 3rd Battery of the 1st Assault Tank Battalion had to leave its Zrínyi to the 10th Assault Tank Battalion (which was stationed in Transylvania) before being sent to Hungary at the end of September.

▲ Image of a Soviet KV-1 knocked out by the Hungarians.

▲ Mercedes Benz L 3000 vehicles and a T-34/76 captured in 1942.

The numerical superiority of the Romanian troops was evident when they succeeded in blocking the Hungarian advance, forcing the Magyars to retreat behind the Maros river where they formed a defensive line whose main strongholds were the towns of Torda and Aranyosegerbegy (Viișoara). This defensive line was already protected by three battalions of the 25th Magyar Infantry Division and was backed by the Maros River for most of its course and flanked on the northern side by 60-80 metre high hills in the valley of the same river.
On the 10th, after the initial breakthrough, the Hungarian armoured troops were sent into reserve only to be called into combat a few days later (13 September) at Torda, where the Hungarians had a strong defensive line. On that very day, the 5th Guard Armoured Corps fell back behind the retreating Hungarian troops near Alsószentmihály (Mihai Viteazu), west of Torda, creating a panic situation for the Hungarian troops. From then on, due to its strategic importance, the 2nd Armoured Division was used as a mobile force ready to be sent to the most needed areas of the front. The new Soviet armoured troops attacked from the left flank of the city, but thanks to their enormous resources from 13-14 September, they were able to extend their offensive towards the western part of the city. In the meantime, the Hungarian armoured troops tried to fill the gaps created by the Soviets in their battered defence system, so between 13 and 14 September the 25th Assault Tank Battalion succeeded with its 75 mm 40M (Pak 40) anti-tank guns in destroying three Soviet tanks and a rocket launcher (possibly a Katiusha), as well as damaging at least seven other tanks. Only a day later, the men of the 25th Tank Battalion would be involved in the fighting in the streets of Torda.
On 15 September, the Soviet High Command ordered Marshal Malinovsky to advance on the Kolozsvár (Cluj-Napoca) - Beszterce (Bistrița) line to put an end to German and Hungarian resistance in Transylvania; and from there to attack north-east to link up with the troops of the 4th Ukrainian Front in the Carpathians.

On 15 September, the Soviets launched their first attack on the town of Torda after intensive artillery preparation. Due to the violence of the attack, the 26th Hungarian Infantry Regiment had to retreat in an orderly manner, leaving the attackers free in the eastern part of Torda. Given the critical situation, the 3rd Battalion, led by its Panther Company, carried out a successful counterattack on 15 September. In particular, the Company led by Taczay initiated this attack in the eastern part of Torda without waiting for the arrival of the rest of his battalion and infantry units, managing in this surprise manoeuvre to destroy three enemy anti-tank guns and two infantry companies. The overwhelming superiority of the enemy allowed Tarczay's Company to be surrounded, but thanks to the courageous action of the Hungarian tanks it managed to avoid encirclement after destroying at least three tanks and one anti-tank gun. On 16 September, the Hungarian 2nd Armoured Division and the 25th Infantry Division launched a counter-attack in a southerly direction between Sósfürdő and elevation 367 to eliminate the enemy bridgehead.

On 17 September, the 6th Motorised Rifle Battalion launched an attack against an enemy bridgehead east of Torda. On its own initiative, Tarczay's Panther Company joined the attack, managing to destroy at least two T-34s. On the same day, the 25th Magyar Infantry Regiment, together with a combat group of the 2nd Armoured Division, launched another counterattack. But once again the stubborn resistance of the enemy, supported in large part by the enormous artillery force, allowed the Hungarians to be held off and a strip of ground east of the Torda bridgehead to be preserved.

The next few days passed with a certain calm as both sides reassembled their troops, interrupted only by artillery attacks, but without the Soviets losing control of their bridgehead.

▲ Hungarian soldiers look curiously at a Panther tank. It is not known whether this vehicle belonged to the Germans or the Hungarians.

More intense fighting took place on 22 September, when combined Soviet and Romanian forces attempted to penetrate through the Magyar defence lines. After an impressive artillery preparation, at 8 a.m. the 180th Rifle Division supported by riflemen of the 5th Guards Armoured Corps with about 30-40 T-34s launched an attack between Sósfürdő and the Szent János valley. At the same time, the 4th Guards Rifle Division attacked with three regiments to the east of the local railway line, having their eastern flank covered by the 7th Romanian Infantry Division. In front of them, the opponent preparing to retaliate was the 2nd Armoured Division. Once again, Tarczay's Panther Company (at that time with only two Panthers in fighting condition) acted alone, launching a counterattack that halted the enemy advance, destroying an infantry battalion and forcing it to retreat. Here Taczay destroyed two T-34s with his tank, although his vehicle was damaged and rendered useless and he had to switch to another Panther to continue the fight.

As a consideration, and before focusing on further fighting, the 10th Tank Assault Battalion consisted of the 1st and 2nd Batteries (with 10 Zrínyi each) and the 3rd Battery (with Turán). In the afternoon of 22 September, the 1st Infantry Battalion, reinforced by the 2nd Battery of the 10th Tank Assault Battalion, launched a successful counterattack against the enemy that surprised the Soviets. As the Soviets advanced through Sósfürdő (north-east of Torda), the six available Zrínyi from the 2nd Battery under the command of Second Lieutenant János Bozsoki were sent to block the road to Sósfürdő to prevent the enemy's advance. Taking advantage of the terrain, Bozsoki placed his six vehicles on the sides of the road, across a valley, in an ambush position. They then only had to wait for the arrival of the Soviet armoured vehicles, and when they arrived, they started firing at them when the first of them was only 50 metres away. The effect of the Zrinyi at such close range was devastating. Within a couple of minutes, they managed to destroy 18 Soviet T-34s for the loss of one Zrinji. In the same

▲ Another Panther tank. Although it is documented that the Hungarians made limited use of it, no photos of Panther tanks under Magyar command are known.

engagement, Bozsoki managed to free a group of Magyar soldiers who had been surrounded by the Soviets, but at that moment the rest of the vehicles in his battery were attacked by much superior forces that put them out of action. Bozsoki did not give up on his comrades and that same night, alone and on foot, he headed for the position to find four wounded crewmen and two Zrínyi still in fighting condition. He placed the wounded inside one of the Zrínyi and drove the vehicle back to his lines to deliver them to the medical teams. But instead of being satisfied that he had done his duty, he set off again on foot to try to get the other operational Zrinyi back to his lines, which he managed to do without the Soviets intervening. After these battles, Bozsoki, who commanded the Zrínyi of the 2nd Battery of the 10th Tank Battalion, was awarded the gold medal for valour for his courageous behaviour, which prevented the Soviets from ending the siege on the town of Torda that day, driving the Soviets out of the town of Sósfürdő. However, the Magyars knew it was only a matter of time before the town fell into enemy hands.

On 23 September at Vaskapu and Sósfar, east-northeast of Torda, the German 23rd Panzer Division arrived with two grenadier panzer regiments and about 65 tanks. Thanks to this appearance, the sector managed to maintain a certain degree of stability, allowing the Axis troops involved in the fighting around Torda to retreat.

On 24 September, only 2 Panther, 6 Pz IV H and 9 Turán of the 3rd Tank Regiment remained in combat condition and were sent to the reserve at Nagy-Ördöngös. On 25 September, the number of armoured vehicles in the reserve was increased by receiving 3 Panther and 3 Tiger after repairs, which were reintegrated into their original companies.

The 6th Motorised Rifle Battalion and the 2nd Motorised Engineer Battalion, supported by 9 Turans and 2 Panthers (the only Panther company left in service), led a counterattack against the Russians in the Péterlakas Valley on 26 September.

On 4 October new Soviet attacks were repeated from the west, causing the front line to move east of the Torda - Kolozsvár road. East of Torda the Soviet tanks advanced in such a way that by the evening of the same day they had almost completed the encirclement of Torda. That "almost" is due to the fact that General Veress managed to maintain a narrow corridor at the southern edge of the town through which he was able to withdraw his troops, leaving the town of Torda permanently abandoned.

The situation became desperate and the troops stationed in Transylvania had to be withdrawn as of 8 October. On the same date, Colonel General Veress ordered the historic capital of Transylvania, Kolozsvár (Cluj), to be abandoned without a fight. This retreat was used by the Romanians to capture Apahira (east of Kolozsvár), where they clashed violently with the Hungarian army on 11 October. The Battle of Torda was a great massacre for the armoured troops between destroyed and captured vehicles. As for the latter, the Romanians took several Toldi, Turán, two Hetzer and at least one Zrínyi.

On 8 October Hitler was forced to allow the Hungarian and German troops on the Maros River to retreat and then take up position behind the Nagyvárad (Oradea Mare) - Szeged (Segedin) line. But the defence that the Axis troops managed to put in place was so weak that on the 10th the Soviets had already reached Szeged, without immediately capturing it due to the ongoing peace talks in Moscow between Hungarian and Soviet representatives.

Between 15 September and 5 October 1944, in the Torda area, Panther Company destroyed

▲ The magnificent Hungarian-made Nimród self-propelled anti-aircraft gun was one of the Hungarian army's most prized vehicles for its versatility.

11 tanks, 17 anti-tank guns, 20 machine guns, a rocket launcher and a multitude of infantry troops. The Battle of Torda was probably the greatest operational success of the Magyar troops, as the ultimate goal of the Soviets and their Romanian allies was to encircle as many Axis troops as possible in an attempt to annihilate Army Group South. The battle for the town of Torda delayed this attempt and thus prevented it to a large extent.

The fighting continued unabated in Magyar territory and on 25 October Tarczay fought near Tiszapolgár, while the Magyar troops were in continuous retreat. There he captured three anti-tank guns and destroyed two T-34s in an ambush, thanks to the high degree of efficiency Tarczay and his men had achieved in handling the formidable Panther. In addition, between 6 and 25 October, his company destroyed five more tanks. On 30 October, south of Tizsapolgár, the Hungarian General Staff and Tarczay's men were surrounded by the enemy vanguard. Confusion reigned on the battlefield, but Tarczay once again demonstrated his fighting skills, despite the fact that his vehicle ended up in a minefield and at the mercy of enemy anti-tank fire from a distance of no more than 25 metres. Within seconds, Tarczay ordered his driver to drive the Panther into the anti-tank and rammed it, eliminating the entire enemy battery.

BATTLES FOR SOUTHERN HUNGARY: ARAD, TISZA, SZENTES

After the Romanian defection, the Hungarian IV Corps was organised to block the advance of Soviet and Romanian forces into the plains of southern Hungary at Arad and Lippa. The IV Corps was united with the VII Corps and redesignated as III Army, commanded by Lieutenant General Heszlényi.

One of the constituent units of the IV Corps was the 1st Armoured Division, on which much of the IV Corps' potential was based. The 3rd Army troops were deployed in the Makóp-Nagyvárad area on 17 September 1944. The 1st Armoured Division was not yet at its theoretical maximum armoured vehicle capacity, as part of its armament was to be ceded to the 2nd Armoured Division to complete the unit. The 1st Armoured Division was again mobilised in August 1944, consisting of the 1st Tank Regiment, which in turn had battalions 1/I and 1/III, the 1st Motorised Rifle Regiment, a reconnaissance battalion and other smaller units. They were also supported by a rocket launcher and two artillery battalions. The reconnaissance battalion had an armoured company, a motorbike company and a motorised company. The unit was formed in August 1944 in view of the imminent need for deployment to the front.

▲ A Nimród participating in an anti-aircraft fire exercise, although it will soon prove its worth as an anti-tank weapon.

▲ Not excellent quality but valuable picture of a StuG III of the 7th Tank Battalion in action.

▼ A captured Hungarian StuG III with painted Soviet identification numbers.

In the autumn of 1944, the 1st Tank Regiment did not yet have its own tanks. The 1st Assault Cannon Battalion and the emerging 2nd-8th Assault Tank Battalions handed over 24 Turan 75s to the 1st Tank Regiment. The 1st Motorised Rifle Regiment also had no vehicles, with the exception of a few Botond 38M guns, so it was necessary to use civilian buses to transport the troops.

On 2 September, the 1st Division had one tank battalion (the 1/III) with 5 Toldis in the command company, three medium tank companies (with 7 Turans, 5 Tolds and 3 Nimrods per company); the 1st Motorised Rifle Regiment had 9 Nimrods, while the 51st Semi-Propelled Anti-Aircraft Artillery Battalion had two Tolds in command, 18 Nimrod and 3 Toldi.

The 1st Armoured Division had a total of about 60-70 armoured vehicles in September 1944. Due to pressure from the Germans, the Hungarian troops attacked on 13 September, advancing from the right flank of the front from the Makó and Gyula region in the direction of Arad, but two infantry divisions and one Romanian cavalry division were waiting for the advance. The objective, as already mentioned, was to capture the town of Arad and advance through the Maros valley towards the Zsil valley with the intention of contacting the Hungarian 2nd Army, with the Hungarian 4th and 7th Corps in charge of accomplishing this. The commander-in-chief of the 3rd Army asked the 1st Armoured Division to support the infantry in this attack. At first they succeeded in advancing at the expense of the Romanian cavalry, with the Turks destroying large enemy cavalry formations on the Macsa-Kürtös road and occupying the town of Arad at dusk on 13 September with all its bridges intact (the Romanians did not try to defend the town at all costs, preferring instead to retreat to their defensive lines on the Maros river). On this occasion, the Romanians could not get maximum help from the Soviets from the start, because their offensive effort required most of their troops in Bulgaria. The capture of Arad can be considered the last completely independent operation of the Magyars during the Second World War.

The vehicles of the 1st Reconnaissance Battalion reached the Maros Valley the following day, where they encountered a Romanian defensive line. Between 14 and 17 September, the 1st Armoured Division fought against the Romanian 19th Infantry Division, managing to break through the line by 16 September, only to be held back 24 hours later by Romanian-backed Soviet armoured units. On 18 September, however, the Magyars managed to reach the slopes of the Carpathians, but were stopped by the stubborn resistance of the Romanian and Soviet troops. A counter-attack by an armoured corps and the Soviet 53rd Army forced the Magyars to retreat towards the Dombegyháza-Battonya line. In these battles, 23 Turán and Toldi vehicles were lost to enemy fire.

The second half of September saw an increase in bombardment of the country by the Soviets, British and Americans, which severely damaged infrastructure, roads, etc. On 20 September, a joint Soviet-Romanian attack supported by 40-50 tanks broke the Hungarian defensive line and the 1st Armoured Division had to return from reserve to support its infantrymen. In the area of Lippa and Máriaradna the 1st Armoured Division supported a Hungarian counter-offensive with the support of the 7th Assault Cannon Battalion, which provided 18 StuG IIIs; they were also supported from the air by a group of German Stukas. Together they managed to destroy, in what became known as the 'Battle of the Pénzespuszta Tanks', around 100 Soviet armoured vehicles, including at least 28 T-34s. On the Hungarian side, several Toldi and Turán were lost under enemy fire. This minor Hungarian success only succeeded in slowing down the Soviet advance, not stopping it, but at least it allowed the units of the 3rd Army to retreat to new defensive positions.

Thus on the 22nd Arad was recaptured by the Soviet-Romanians, only three days after the city of Temesvár (Timisoara) had also been taken a little further south, ending the Soviet offensive in western Transylvania on 25 October 1944.

The defensive structure in Southern Hungary was the responsibility of Army Group South, under the command of General Johannes Friessner. This comprised the Hungarian 2nd Army (commanded by General Jeno Major), which included the Hungarian 2nd Armoured Division, the Hungarian 3rd Army (commanded by General József Heszlény), which included the Hungarian 1st Armoured Division, and the German 6th Army (commanded by General Maximiliam Fretter-Pico). The defensive troops numbered about 80,000 men (50,000 Hungarians and 30,000 Germans), 300 armoured vehicles, 3,500 cannons and about 500 aircraft. The German 6th Army included units that, although diminished in their potential, would still be a very tough opponent for the Soviets to deal with, such as the 1st, 13th and 23rd Panzer Divisions, the 'Felherrnhalle' Panzer-Granatier Division and the tanks of the 503rd Heavy Armoured Battalion.

Against them, the Soviets and Romanians of the 2nd Ukrainian Front deployed about 260000 men (200000 Soviets and 60000 Romanians), 825 armoured vehicles, over 10,000 cannons and about 1000 aircraft. They were part of 10 armies (8 Soviet and 2 Romanian): VIIth Guard Army, VIth Armoured Guard Army, XVIIth, XLth and LIIIth Armies, the mechanised cavalry groups "Pliyev" and "Gorshkov", reserve troops, as well as the 1st and 4th Romanian Armies.

In the period 20-22 September, the 3rd Army was reorganised, with German troops from the 4th SS Panzer-Granatier Division and the 22nd SS Cavalry Division 'Maria Theresa' being assigned. Between 20 and 22 September, the Soviets lost about 70 armoured vehicles in the fighting against the Hungarian infantry (8th and 20th Divisions) and tanks. On 22 September, the Soviets had the vast Hungarian plain in front of them.

On 25 September the 2nd battery of the 7th Assault Cannon Battalion, commanded by 1st Lieutenant Köszeghy and supported by infantry, took Csanádpalota. The StuG IIIs destroyed 4 T-34s, 4 anti-tank guns and 13 trucks. Despite this initial success, the Hungarians were ordered to retreat on the evening of 26 September. During this retreat, they were ambushed by Soviet T-34s of the 18th Tank Corps and Su-85s of the 1438th Artillery Regiment with self-propelled guns. In these clashes, 1st Lieutenant Köszeghy's vehicle was damaged. With his famous vehicle bearing the number 700 in black (the 7th Battalion commander's own number), he continued to fight with great bravery and outnumbered, managing to destroy several T-34s before they were hit and destroyed by enemy fire. The loss of the commander demoralised the rest of his men, leaving several intact StuG IIIs abandoned on the battlefield. Three of these assault guns were later recovered in a Hungarian rescue manoeuvre. The final result of the ambush was the loss of nine StuG IIIs and 12 T-34s.

At 04:00 on 6 October, the 2nd Ukrainian Front began a major offensive in Hungary, starting from the city of Arad and supported by a huge number of troops and armoured vehicles to be deployed between the Danube and Tisza rivers. The units constituting the 2nd Ukrainian

Front were three mechanised army corps, three cavalry corps and seventeen rifle divisions. Marshal Malinovsky planned to break the Magyar defences in that sector (the 3rd Magyar Army), so he ordered the 6th Guard Armoured Army and General Pliev's Mechanised Cavalry Group (consisting of a cavalry corps, an armoured corps and a mechanised corps) into action. The intention was to send his forces, once the front was broken, in a northerly direction, to pocket the German-Hungarian troops still defending northern Transylvania. The advance was lightning fast and met little opposition, allowing them to penetrate about 60 kilometres behind enemy lines on the first day. But one day later the 1st and 23rd Panzer Divisions, supported by German infantry troops, managed to stop the Soviet advance about 10 kilometres behind the town of Oradea, also in present-day Romanian territory.

Another 'guest' in the aforementioned battles was the 1st Cavalry Division, which after its return from Germany in October-November 1944 and subsequent reorganisation was employed in the defence of the motherland. Although it is true that its component units had to be dispersed in the Magyar defence network, some of them played an important role in the fighting in Szentes. In particular, the 2nd Hussar Regiment of 7 October 1944 was sent to the bridgehead of Szentes to defend the retreating Hungarian troops. There, the 75-mm Pak 40s of the 2nd Anti-Tank Company achieved several victories over enemy armoured vehicles. Also during the fighting at the Szentes bridgehead in October 1944, most of the 7th Assault Cannon Battalion was destroyed. The remains of the battalion fled in the direction of Budapest, where they were integrated into the 'Billnitzer' Group. The Battalion destroyed at least 67 tanks and 14 vehicles of various types during the clashes with the Soviets in the Tisza River area (with the loss of 8 StuG IIIs destroyed, 10 badly damaged and 12 lightly damaged). On 8 October, having not yet suspended the attack due to the ongoing armistice negotiations with Hungary, the Soviet troops reached the Tisza River.

Another tank battalion that took part in the fighting in the Szentes area was the 13th, although it was only able to do so with the two Turán 75s it had available for training its troops. The rest of the battalion had to fight on foot. Like the men of the 10th Tank Assault Battalion, those of the 13th Tank Assault Battalion also found their depleted corps in Budapest during the retreat, where they joined the 'Billnitzer' Group as mainly infantry troops. Despite German resistance, Soviet troops crossed the natural Hungarian border in the Szegez sector on 8 October. Attempts by the 23rd Panzer Division to stop the Soviets again were unsuccessful and they were forced to retreat together with other German and Hungarian troops along the road between Szlonok and Debrecen.

Further attempts to hold back the Soviets took place on the 9th, with the 1st and 13th Panzer Divisions attempting to envelop the Red Army advances in an attempt to crush them. Despite this attempt, the 10th saw the Soviet advance into the Magyar lands, the crossing of the Tisza and finally the capture of the village of Kecsment, some 70 kilometres from Budapest. Only the actions of the men of the 22nd SS 'Maria Theresa' Cavalry Division once again succeeded in stopping the Soviet advance.

On 11 October, a counter-offensive of the Axis troops led by the armoured units of the 1st Armoured Division and the Hungarian 23rd Division began, which allowed them to overwhelm the Soviet vanguard in Mindszent, represented by the Soviet 243rd Rifle Division (thus preventing the formation of a bridgehead behind the Tisza River in Mindszent). The Magyar advance allowed the Romanian 4th Infantry Division to be almost completely destroyed on 20 October near Szlonok (this was the third time this happened to this unit during the Second World War). German troops from the 24th Panzer Division, the 4th SS Panzer-Grenadier Division and a Tiger tank battalion took part in the fighting.

The Hungarian thrust was halted on 22 October by Soviet mechanised forces, who in a counter-attack north of the Tisza River managed to push the Hungarians back, leaving them a clear path to Debrecen and Nyíregyháza.

Once again, the 1st Hungarian Cavalry Division, together with the 20th Hungarian Infantry Division, launched an attack on the western bank of the Tisza River on 25 October. In these clashes they first managed to contain and then defeat the Romanian 2nd Infantry Division. Between 26 and 29 the Hungarian 3rd and 8th Infantry Divisions, supported by elements of the 1st Armoured Division, unsuccessfully attempted to eliminate the Alpar bridgehead.

These battles had once again drained the Hungarian troops, so much so that, in an attempt to reorganise them, on 29 October 1944, the remnants of the Hungarian 1st Armoured Division (with about 20 armoured vehicles in combat condition on 31 October) were placed under the command of the German 3rd Panzer Corps in Kecskemét. As an indication of the difficulties of the Hungarian situation, in November 1944, only 10 StuGs of the 7th Assault Cannon Battalion were in reserve with the Hungarian 3rd Army.

▲ The destroyed StuG III of Lieutenant Barnabas Koszeghy, Hungarian assault tank ace. The numbering identifies it as the command vehicle of the 7th Assault Tank Battalion.

DEBRECEN, THE GATEWAY TO BUDAPEST

At the same time as these events at the front, political movements were taking place within Hungary that would determine Hungary's future for the rest of the world conflict. Regent Horthy saw the situation at the front as a complete defeat for Hungary and sought a political solution. Between the end of August and the beginning of September, rumours of peace negotiations spread, confirmed on 15 October by an attempt at an armistice with the Soviet Union and a break with Germany; but the Hungarian army could not afford to neglect the fight against the Soviet hordes approaching from the east, so it completely ignored any attempt at an armistice. The Germans, for their part, were aware of Horthy's moves and his subsequent declaration, and their reaction was immediate, aided by the supporters of the Hungarian National Socialist 'Arrow Cross' party, who were firmly opposed to such an armistice. This reaction immediately materialised in the so-called 'Panzerfaust' operation.

The events of this operation unfolded as follows. On 15 October, an SS commando led by Otto Skorzeny was sent to Budapest and simultaneously kidnapped Nicholas Horthy (the regent's son). In the event that the armistice was realised and turned the Hungarians against the Germans (as had happened in Bulgaria and Romania), Skorzeny's men, supported by four Königstiger tanks and other German troops, headed for Buda Castle (the seat of Hungarian power) to conquer it. Some of the Hungarian troops protecting the castle exchanged fire until they surrendered to the Germans. After these events in Budapest and the kidnapping of his son, Horthy retracted his attempt at an armistice, accepting his resignation as regent and subsequent imprisonment.

After Horthy's dismissal, the pro-German count Ferenc Szálasi, leader of the 'Arrow Cross' party, took his place. Horthy's attempted armistice had slowed down the Soviet advance, but after his failure and the pro-German takeover in Hungary, the Soviet advance continued even more aggressively.

Interestingly, on the day following Horthy's proclamation, General Béla Miklós and his chief of staff, Colonel Kálmán Kéri, passed to the enemy. Together with them, and on Miklós's orders, some 20,000 Magyar soldiers passed to the Soviets of the Fourth Ukrainian Front. Miklós would later join the Hungarian government-in-exile and some of these soldiers would take part in the operations for the Soviet conquest of Budapest.

The situation of the population must be understood as very complicated, as more and more people realised the futility of continuing the war. But for the soldiers of the Hungarian army the dilemma was even more serious, because for most of them neither fascism nor communism were viable alternatives. They had been caught up in the maelstrom of the Second World War and had no choice but to fight for their homeland.

Meanwhile, the battle for Debrecen took place on the front line between 6 and 29 October. Here, the Germans, supported by the Hungarians, attempted for the umpteenth time to stop the Soviets of Malinovsky's 2nd Ukrainian Front and their Romanian allies, this time attempting to crush Hungary's eastern defences. A Soviet cavalry group managed to penetrate the Hungarian defences and penetrate deep into the country, managing to cut through the traffic between Szolnok and Debrecen, and then reach Debrecen.

▲ 1944 propaganda poster of Szálasi and his Arrow Cross party.

But there they ran into a powerful German force that was concentrating to participate in the counter-offensive called Operation 'Zigeunerbaron' ('Zigeunerbaron' in German), which was supposed to drive the Soviets out of the Southern Carpathians by conquering the mountain passes and which was to begin on 12 October (as we can see, the Soviets unknowingly beat the Germans in this action).

The 16th Tank Assault Battalion was one of the armoured units that would take part in the fight for the defence of Debrecen alongside the German troops. Although this unit was theoretically supposed to be composed of some type of assault tank, it had to be equipped with the Turan 75s it had used during the training period due to the shortage of resources. Ten Turan 75s and two Turan 40s had arrived from the surplus of the 1st Tank Battalion after it had been equipped with the Zrinyi.

The tanks of the 16th Assault Battalion found themselves defending the entrances to the city of Debrecen on 10 October against T-34 and Soviet cavalry and infantry troops. Despite their obvious inferiority to the enemy armoured vehicles, the Turans managed to contain the cavalry assault. But behind them, 14 T-34s advanced against the Magyars, who, well planted on the ground, managed to destroy an enemy armoured vehicle and hold their positions in exchange for the loss of three Turan 75s. But the immense Soviet superiority was again demonstrated when, a few hours later, 45 T-34s attacked the Magyars en masse, forcing the tanks of the 16th Tank Battalion to retreat to better defensive positions.

On 11 October, Soviet cavalry troops reached the outskirts of Debrecen. In response to this imminent danger, a counter-attack was immediately launched by German infantry and tank troops of the 23rd Panzer Division, as well as the omnipresent tanks of the 16th Tank Assault Battalion. This rapid intervention allowed the enemy cavalry to be driven out of the city and re-established the defensive line in the southern part of Debrecen.

The increasing Soviet pressure led to continuous clashes between troops on both sides. Thus, on 13 October, some of the surviving tanks of the 16th Assault Battalion, which were positioned to defend the railway area along the Szolnok road, were again attacked by Soviet cavalry. Supported by a unit of German engineers, they again managed to repel the attack with heavy Soviet losses. Some other tanks of the 16th Assault Tank Battalion, which had been positioned in the western region of the defensive perimeter of Debrecen, also managed to fight back. Another Soviet attack was repulsed by Hungarian tanks, this time supported by Hungarian and German anti-aircraft guns used as anti-aircraft artillery.

The next day, 14 October, the Turán 75s belonging to the 1st and 2nd batteries of the 16th Assault Tank Battalion moved towards Gyula to face another Soviet cavalry attack, which they routed with some ease.

While it was true that the ongoing war of attrition was causing a high number of casualties among the attackers, it was also true that the defenders could hardly recover their losses, while the Soviet arsenal of men and vehicles seemed inexhaustible. Consequently, despite numerous successes in the defence of Debrecen, the 16th Tank Battalion was ordered to retreat in the direction of Polgár (along the Tisza River) on 19 October, having lost no less than 600 men and much of its armoured equipment. Initially, Pliev Group did not participate in the capture of Debrecen because it was sent in the direction of Oradea (Nagyvárad for the Hungarians) to surprise the German-Hungarian defenders who were still holding off the 6th Armoured Guard Army from the rear. This manoeuvre proved decisive, as the defenders were caught in the crossfire and could only retreat from the city of Debrecen. After the retreat of the Magyars, between the 19th and 20th, three Romanian divisions finally took power in Debrecen after a joint assault.

The Battle of Debrecen had ended in a tactical victory for the Soviets and Romanians, who had also suffered a huge number of human and material losses, but the Soviet pressure on the battered Axis troops was far from over, as their advance continued. During the battle for Debrecen, until 20 October, hundreds of tanks and armoured assault vehicles fought between the two sides. The intensity of the fighting led to the exhaustion of the defending troops, who were reluctant to be encircled by the Soviets. Both the Germans and Hungarians withdrew without delay behind the protection of the Tisza River in an attempt to avoid encirclement. Faced with this movement, the Pliev Group launched an attack on Nyíregyháza, where they took control of the various river crossing points. Nyíregyháza witnessed one of the fiercest battles of those days, until it was finally conquered by the Soviets between 21 and 30 October 1944. After conquering Nyíregyháza on 21 October, the Soviets were surrounded by German-Hungarian troops retreating from Debrecen and northern Transylvania, who were decimated until they managed to break the siege. The city finally fell to the Soviets on 30 October.

During the battle for Debrecen and all the fighting in the area, the resolute and courageous action of the German and Hungarian troops caused heavy losses among the attackers (estimated at over 110,000 men, 500 armoured vehicles and about 1,500 artillery pieces). For their part, the defenders suffered at least 20,000 casualties, as well as countless other military means.

After winning the Battle of Debrecen, the Soviet troops and their Romanian allies proceeded to eliminate all German and Magyar formations still active in northern Transylvania. The objective was to reach the river Tisza and, from there, gain access to the Hungarian plain so suitable for the movement of their armoured troops. Although the Soviets succeeded in getting Malinovsky's troops to conquer the entire region (Tiszántúl), the Marshal could not be satisfied with allowing more than 150,000 German and Hungarian troops to retreat and reach the defensive lines across the Tisza river. Unfortunately for the Germans and Hungarians, the defensive line along the Tisza was not fully fortified. Therefore, it was only a matter of time before the 2nd Ukrainian Front, despite the heavy losses suffered in the fighting in the Nagyvárad-Debrecen-Nyíregyháza area, decided to continue its march towards Budapest, which it did.

Between 23 and 24 October, a German counterattack on the town of Nagykálló temporarily halted the Soviet advance.

The Soviets were advancing from all directions on the diminishing territory of the Reich and its Hungarian ally. Thus, at the same time as the above-mentioned events, in the second half of October, the 1st Ukrainian Front and the 4th Ukrainian Front were involved in the attack on the region of Ruthenia and Slovakia. Towards the end of October, coinciding with the capture of Mukachevo on the 26th and Uzhorod on the 27th, Ruthenia was finally conquered by the Red Army.

▲ The German-built Sdfkz 8 half-track made a great contribution to Hungary as a heavy artillery tractor. Pictured here is one in action at Kerepes.

▼ One of the few Sd.Kfz.251/8 half-tracks in a sanitary version available to the Hungarian army.

Despite the slight slowdown caused to the Soviet vanguards by the Battle of Nagykálló, the Red Army finally began its offensive against Budapest on 29 October (under direct orders from Stalin, who was in a hurry to take the Magyar capital), with over 100,000 men in two attack groups converging on the Hungarian capital to isolate it from the German and Hungarian forces still in the country.

Meanwhile, during the second half of November 1944, reinforcements continued to arrive in small steps in the form of men and vehicles for the 2nd Armoured Division, which were delivered near Párkány (Sturovo, Slovakia). The 3rd Tank Regiment came into possession of nine Pz IV H and two Toldi, and the Turán crews were also prepared for their imminent conversion into the more powerful Pz IV.

Elements of the Hungarian Horváth Battle Group, led by Lieutenant Colonel Horváth, fought at Perbál with two Turán, one Toldi and four Nímrod. This same group with 11 tanks, together with the remnants of the 7th Tank Assault Battalion and with the support of the 2nd Hussar Regiment, carried out a counter-attack on 7 December at Baracska-Petend (the following day it was the 10th Tank Assault Battalion that entered the battle, although this will be discussed in the chapter on the siege of Budapest). In the heavy fighting between 28 October and 9 December, both sides were materially exhausted.

On 10 December the Horváth Group had only two 40M Turán. The remains of the 7th Tank Battalion fought on 11 September at Gárdony-Kisvelence.

▲ Hungarian soldiers surround a captured Soviet T-34/75. Few were able to be pressed into service against their original owners.

For its part, the 2nd Armoured Division engaged in several battles as part of the attempt to avoid the encirclement of Budapest, near Ipolyság (supported by a regiment of the infamous SS Sturmbrigade Dirlewanger), which finally fell on 14 December 1944 and continued between 9 and 19 December with further fighting at Lovasbéreny. At the beginning of December, the division was almost decimated, with about 119 armoured vehicles, but only 17 fit for service at the front: 26 40M Nímrod, 8 39M Csaba, 35 40M Turán 40, 8 41M Turán 75, 16 38M Toldi, 1 Pz III, 20 Pz IV H, 4 Panther and 1 StuG III. By the end of the month, however, more than 100 of these vehicles had been completely withdrawn from service (in fact, as of 21 December, only 2 Panther and 2 PZ IV H of German origin remained in combat condition in the 2nd Armoured Division).

On 25 December, the Soviet 170th Armoured Brigade was momentarily halted in its advance south-east of Dorog by German anti-aircraft guns supported by some Hungarian assault tanks, which resulted in the destruction of four T-34s. Later that afternoon, Dorog finally fell into Soviet hands.

On 26 December 1944, the Russian offensive began with the capture of Dunahararezti-Soroksar, followed by clashes at Vecses, Rakoszaba and Horthy Bridge.

In addition to the actual fighting, the conflict extended to the political sphere: on 28 December 1944, the Soviets promoted an unsuccessful attempt to legitimise a new Hungarian government led by Béla Miklós in the Magyar territory controlled by the Red Army against the Szálasy government.

▲ A Hetzer captured by the Soviets who put their marks on it.

THE SIEGE OF BUDAPEST

As already mentioned, the offensive against the Hungarian capital began on 29 October and by 7 November, the Soviets had reached the suburbs of the Hungarian capital some 20 kilometres away.

The 3rd Ukrainian Front, after completing operations in Yugoslavia, moved north with Hungary in its sights. Between 7 and 9 November, they crossed the Danube at Batina and Apatin and established a bridgehead across the river. Once the bridgeheads were reinforced, they launched an offensive against the Magyar territory. Faced with such a powerful attack, the Hungarians and Germans decided to retreat to reinforce their positions on the 'Margit' line. This defensive line was the best prepared and fortified line in Hungary and ran along the Danube - Budapest - Erd - Lake Velence - Lake Balaton - Nagybajom. The 'Margit' line was held to the north by the Hungarian 2nd Army and the German 8th Army, while between Érd and Lake Balaton the Hungarian 3rd Army and the German 6th Army were fortified. The desperate situation was also exploited to disable the Hungarian 2nd Army on 13 November, sending its remnants to join the 1st and 3rd Armies.

Initially the fighting was intense, but from 9 December it subsided as preparations began for the encirclement of Budapest from the west. The innermost ring of the encirclement would be made by the Soviet 46th Army (which attacked north of Lake Velencei), while the outer ring of the encirclement would be made southwest of the lake by the 4th Guard Army; from there they would reach the Danube at Komárom.

▲ Part of the Erzsébet Bridge, in Pest, demolished to make it more difficult for the Soviets to cross.

From that point there was a short period of reorganisation of the attackers before the final assault on the city, which began on 19 December. At the beginning of December the Soviets reached the Pest suburbs, reaching the Ipoly-Danube line to the north (remember that in the previous chapter we discussed the actions of the 2nd Magyar Armoured Division in this area). At this point the offensive of the 2nd Ukrainian Front came to a halt because they received orders to wait for the 3rd Ukrainian Front. So they had to wait for the 3rd Ukrainian Front to reorganise after the first attacks against the "Margit" line. As a curiosity, one of the forces that participated in these battles was the Buda Volunteer Regiment, composed of Hungarians who had changed sides. Starting on the 19th, the Soviet and Romanian advance accelerated to such an extent that within a single week they managed to complete the encirclement of the capital after cutting the road that still connected Vienna to Budapest, leaving some 33,000 German soldiers, 37,000 Hungarian soldiers (of the I Corps with the 1st Armoured Division, the 1st Hussar Cavalry Division, remnants of several tank battalions and other units of lesser potential) and 800,000 civilians inside. The possibility of escape for these hundreds of thousands practically disappeared because on 23 November 1944 Budapest was declared a fortress (Festung) by Hitler, which had to be defended to the last at any cost. For this purpose, from that November 1944, a series of parapets and easily defensible areas were created within the so-called Attila lines. The Attila Defence Lines consisted of three defensive rings on the outskirts of Pest, another on the outskirts of Pest and a third ring inside Pest. After Attila's lines, six more lines were created by the defenders within the city (these lines were semicircular in shape and followed the route of the city's various avenues and boulevards, even though they were only temporary fortifications supported by electrified barbed wire and minefields; these six defensive lines were characterised by the fact that they all began and ended at the Danube). The Buda area, being further west, did not have the same protection as Pest, which the city's defenders soon 'paid for'.

Elements of the 1st Armoured Division and the Hussar Division, together with 6 tank battalions and other Hungarian and German troops, were besieged in Budapest on 23 November 1944. Among the German troops were the remnants of the 13th Panzer Division, the 60th Panzer Grenadier Division 'Feldherrnhalle', the 8th SS Cavalry Division 'Florian Geyer' and the 22nd SS Volunteer Cavalry Division 'Maria Theresia', which formed the main support that enabled them to withstand the initial Soviet assault on the Hungarian capital.

The 1st Armoured Division had seven tanks, three anti-tank guns and little else, its main contribution was men (about 5,000); the 1st Hussar Division had only four armoured vehicles. The 6 assault tank battalions led by Lieutenant General Ernö Billnitzer (head of the assault tank training camp) in the so-called 'Billnitzer Group' had a total of about 30 assault tanks (StuG III, Zrinyi and Hetzer) and 8 75 mm anti-tank guns. As there were more troops than vehicles, many of the crews were used as infantry troops. The Zrínyi and Hetzer were well suited, due to their low profile and powerful armament, to the street fighting that awaited them; and they would prove this in Budapest despite their frank inferiority to the Soviets.

The "Billnitzer" Group consisted of the remnants of the battalions that had withdrawn from the front towards the city, i.e. the 1st, 7th, 10th and parts of the 13th, 16th and 25th (according to some historians, a battery of the 20th, equipped with Hetzers, and remnants of the 24th with

5 Turans, 2 Toldi and 22 Hetzers should also be added). Some newly manufactured Zrínyi from the Ganz factory in the same town were also added to this group. The 1st Battery of the 3rd Assault Tank Battalion had 5 Zrinyi and some Turan, the 7th Battalion had four or five StuG III, the 1st Battery of the 10th Assault Tank Battalion had 11 Zrinyi and some trucks. These vehicles were obviously too few for the task of defending Budapest with any chance of success, so they were often used in small groups of two or three vehicles as a mobile reserve to go to the most vulnerable areas.

Between 5 November and 8 December, the hussars of what remained of the 1st Cavalry Division took up defensive positions on Csepel Island in the southern part of Budapest. This was where much of the capital's industrial heart was located. Intense fighting between factories allowed the production of artillery ammunition, panzerfaust, small arms and even some armoured vehicles, as in the case of the Manfred Weiss site, to continue to the last. Most of the 4th Hussar Regiment and the 2nd Artillery Battalion were encircled inside Budapest, while the remaining disbanded units that managed to avoid the Hungarian capital finally managed to surrender to the American army in Austria in March 1945.

The 10th Tank Assault Battalion led a counter-attack against a Soviet bridgehead in Baracska on 8 December 1944. The attack, which started between Baracska and Martonvásár, succeeded in pushing the Soviets back almost as far as the Danube north of Ercsi. A battery of the 1st Tank Battalion took part in this attack (without any orders to do so). In this engagement, 15 Soviet anti-tank tanks were destroyed or captured, killing about 250 of their opponents. This courageous attack succeeded in 'calming' the area for a few days and even

▲ A Turán II runs through the streets of Budapest.

allowed the action of the Hungarians to be mentioned in German reports that emphasised their bravery. Only three days later, on 11 December, Lieutenant Rátz's battery of the 1st Tank Assault Battalion and the vehicles of the 10th Tank Assault Battalion were engaged in the streets of the town of Erd, south-west of Budapest.

The armoured forces that fought in Budapest included the Gendarmerie. They had 10 obsolete Ansaldo tanks (withdrawn from the front for years), 10 Toldi and 10 Csaba. They too carried out attacks against Soviet troops at Vecsés on 1 November 1944 with disastrous results, as all Ansaldo tanks were lost in a short time due to Soviet superiority. In another major engagement on 27 December, the Gendarmerie forces were again severely punished and decimated. On the same day, the main airport in Budapest was lost to the Soviets and thus the possibility of receiving the 80 tons of material that the fortress was supposed to receive per day to supply only the troops, not counting civilians.

During November and December, troops belonging to the assault tank battalions, without their mounts, faced the enemy on foot in the Vecsés-Maglad-Ecser area near Pest, accompanying the Hungarian 1st Armoured Division. Despite the pitiful conditions, they managed to temporarily halt the enemy advance, thanks to the limited armoured support they received.

On 23 December, the town of Székesfehérvár fell to the Soviets. On 24 December, three army corps penetrated the defensive positions of the Hungarian 1st Armoured Division between Ecser and Vecsés, south-east of the town, and also initiated a major attack on the Hungarian 10th Division between Csömör and Fót, north-east. Attacks and counter-attacks were repeated along the entire front line, each time recovering and losing a few hundred metres. An example is that of 25 December south of Mogyoród (near Csömör), where

▲ A civilian calmly reads the newspaper on the wreckage of a Zrínyi II of the Billnitzer Group in Budapest in the summer of 1945. The name 'SÁRI' is written on the front of the tank.

the German troops retreated about 500 metres only to be recaptured the same afternoon with the help of two German assault tanks and eight support men (two Magyar companies were captured in this action). That same Christmas Day, the main road to Budapest was cut off by the Soviets, leaving only a secondary road to Esztergom in the direction of the Hungarian capital open, but only for another 24 hours. It was at this precise moment that the units of the 2nd Ukrainian Front and the 3rd Ukrainian Front came into contact, completely closing the encirclement of Budapest.

During the fighting on Attila's first two defence lines, the defenders showed great determination despite their inferiority in men and weapons, although the latter was slightly compensated for by the ubiquitous panzerfausts, which claimed numerous casualties among the armoured men. On 27 December, a Soviet attack aimed at crossing the Danube and conquering the island of Csepel from the east was repulsed by Hungarian anti-aircraft guns (acting against ground targets).

The attack from the east in the direction of Pest put the defenders under increasing pressure. Thus, on 28 December, the bulk of the 'Billnitzer' Group was in position in the Kispest area of the Magyar capital. On the same day, after unsuccessful attempts to stop the enemy offensive, the remnants of the 1st and 13th Magyar Assault Tank Battalions that had been positioned between Pécel and Ferihegy had to retreat after being unable to close the gap left by the retreating 8th SS Cavalry Division "Florian Geyer". Meanwhile, the armoured units of the 16th and 24th Hungarian Tank Battalions managed to hold their positions at Rákoskeresztur and Újmajor. On the same day, the areas east and south-east of Pest, Maglód and Gyál were already in Soviet hands.

On 29 December, the Soviets tried to negotiate the surrender of the capital with the defenders, but were unsuccessful due to Hitler's strict orders and the fact that the jeep carrying the first Soviet deputies exploded, possibly hitting a mine. Due to the rejection of the proposal, the Soviets began to 'prepare' the ground, subjecting it to intense artillery fire (almost a thousand guns) for 7-10 hours on 30-31 December and 1 January, with air strikes taking over during the hours when the artillery was at rest.

Between the end of December 1944 and the beginning of January 1945, the Hungarian tanks fought in the western suburbs of Pest, flanked by the German troops of the 13th Panzer Division and the 22nd SS 'Maria Theresa' Volunteer Cavalry Division, which supported them in several counter-attacks against the Soviets and managed to temporarily hold them off. On 31 December, near Rakóskeresztúr, the armoured units of the 24th Assault Battalion led by Commander Barnabás Bakó managed to repel a Soviet attack, inflicting heavy losses. For their part, the Soviets gradually tightened their grip on the city; in the Buda area the 3rd Ukrainian Front sent the 46th Army (with the 37th and 75th Rifle Corps and the 18th Guard Rifle Corps), while in the Pest area the 2nd Ukrainian Front was assigned to attack with its 7th Army (with the 30th Rifle Corps, the 18th Guard Rifle Corps and the Romanian 7th Corps). Although Operation 'Konrad' to try to liberate Budapest began on 1 January, at the same time as the events we are describing, it is not included in this chapter but in a separate chapter for a better understanding of the events.

On 5 January Soviet tanks were already marching into parts of Pest, although it is true that many parts of the city were still in the hands of the defenders. On the 6th, the Soviets took over the Hofherr-Schrantz factory, the only one still producing spare parts for German-Hungarian armoured vehicles and serving as a repair shop. On the same day, the airstrip on the island of Csepel came under direct Soviet fire and had to be abandoned on the 7th.

On 7 January, the last armoured troops of the 10th Tank Battalion of the "Billnitzer" Group, supported by German troops, attacked the Soviets in an attempt to regain an airfield on an airstrip (after its loss a few days earlier, only the emergency airstrip on the island of Csepel still served as an entry point for supplies, but with enemy fire, it was impossible to use it, as already mentioned). But the Soviet superiority and the low numbers of the attackers' infantry forced him to give up and retreat, even though Billnitzer's armoured units had managed to take up positions on part of the runway.

On the same day, he witnessed at least nine failed counter-attacks in Kőbánya by the men of the 22nd SS Volunteer Cavalry Division 'Maria Theresia', supported by the armoured vehicles of the 'Billnitzer' Group, who eventually had to abandon the district.

The Soviets and Romanians continued to penetrate the defensive lines, but from time to time the defenders inflicted a hard blow on them. Thus, on 8 January, near the Józsefváros station (already on the third defensive line inside Pest), German infantry troops supported by three Zrínyi from the 1st Tank Battalion recaptured a small area of buildings belonging to the National Railway Company (MÁV). On 9 January, German infantry supported by Hungarian tanks retook part of Népliget Park, but Soviet and Romanian pressure led to an order for the defenders of Csepel Island to retreat to Buda, to be completed the following day.

▲ A self-propelled Magyar Zrínyi cannon, which with its 105 mm howitzer proved to be quite effective in street fighting, is visible among the rubble.

On 11 January, there was another attack by Zrínyi's assault tanks, which managed (with the support of the gendarmerie men, who were already acting as pure infantry) to capture the western part of Orczy Square. Within two days, the Soviets would recapture the area, forcing the Hungarians to retreat.

On 14 December, faced with the imminent arrival of the Soviet-Romanian tide in the centre of Pest, the 'Billnitzer' Group was called in to seal off the Grand Boulevard (the fifth line of defence within Pest), with the armoured men still fighting, supported by two engineer battalions and some river assault boats. On the 15th, 7-8 assault guns moved in to successfully repel the Soviets who had reached the National Museum. After creating a series of barricades and conveniently undermining the Boulevard, the Hungarians, supported by their assault tanks, managed to resist the Soviet assault until 17 January. But once again Soviet pressure drove the Hungarians to retreat to Buda after crossing the Danube. The idea was to organise a stronger resistance in Buda, which began with blowing up the five bridges connecting Buda and Pest on 18 January at 7 a.m., to make it more difficult to reach the last stronghold of the defenders (although the only two bridges that held out despite extensive damage were the Erzsébet and Catena bridges). The Billnitzer Group was immediately deployed in the western part of Buda to defend the suburbs of that area from the Soviet advance. The 1st Armoured Division had lost its few armoured vehicles during the fighting and its men acted as infantrymen for the remainder of the encirclement (at the beginning of February it had only 200 men).

▲ Another of the many 'accumulation' sites of military equipment put out of use in Budapest after the fighting. Visible are several T-70 light armoured vehicles and an R-35 of French origin (the latter possibly of Polish origin), used for training Magyar troops at the Academy and deployed for static defence in the Vérmező area.

▲ Another image of combat debris in the streets of Budapest. There were dozens of 'collection' points for weapons after the fighting.

▼ An abandoned Hungarian armoured car at Keleti station, showing an 80 mm artillery piece, a turret anti-tank gun and two machine guns, used in the fighting for Budapest. Hungary had a great interest in armoured trains during the Second World War.

Meanwhile, on 20 January 1945 in Moscow, representatives of the Hungarian Miklós provisional government signed the armistice, although it was of little value in the areas controlled by the Germans and the Szálasi government. In Budapest, of course, it had no value. It must be remembered that, at the same time as the attacks on Pest, the siege on Buda was tightening every day since the end of December 1944, so some of the troops positioned in Pest were transferred to the Buda side. Here the fighting was less intense than in Pest, but there was no lack of actions by the Magyar armoured troops, such as the one on 27 December in which, supported by infantry, they recaptured the Kelenföld station. Soviet pressure continued throughout January to further suffocate the last remaining pockets of defenders on that side of the river. Between 17 and 19 January, gendarmerie troops supported by a Hungarian armoured battle group made a counter-attack in the direction of the Mártonhegyi road. On 25 January, armoured troops of the 'Billnitzer' Group supported by German infantry intervened in the area of the railway tracks in Lágymánios, trying unsuccessfully to seize a uniform factory where many defenders were besieged on the upper floor.

▲ One of the few Hungarian-made Nimród anti-aircraft armoured vehicles that took part in the fighting for Budapest. These armoured vehicles were successfully used in both anti-aircraft and ground combat due to their high rate of fire.

On 5 February, the last seven supply gliders are received and manage to reach the city at Vérmezö (although one crashes on landing), but it is too little for the needs. On 6 February, the Soviets continued their advance on Buda, causing further retreats by the defenders. Shortly afterwards, the Soviets also captured Margaret Island, in the Danube, while passing Budapest (the attacks on this island had begun on 19 January). The next target is the Citadel, which, after falling, leaves the defenders in a confined space of about two square kilometres on Castle Hill, under continuous artillery and bombardment fire.

The desperate situation, with the disappearance of possible outside help after the failure of Operations Konrad I, II and III, led the commander of the square, SS-Obergruppenführer von Wildenbruch, to order on 11 February that the survivors of the encirclement attempt to break the siege. In an attempt to surprise the Soviets and have any chance of success, the siege was broken in three directions. Between 28,000 and 30,000 German and Hungarian soldiers attempted to break through in three columns. Only the first managed to advance for a while under the cover of fog, while the other two were massacred. On the same day, the last Zrínyi still in fighting condition were blown up by their crews in front of the Budapest University of Technology to prevent them from falling intact into Soviet hands.

Thus the remnants of the 'Billnitzer' Group, now without armour, participated in the most successful escape attempt from Castle Hill. Billnitzer himself (recently promoted to lieutenant-general for his numerous actions in defence of the capital) and a small group of men from his tanks broke through Széll Kálmán Square and, despite the Soviet attacks, managed to reach the Törökvész road through which they reached a snowy forest west of Buda, only to be caught shortly afterwards in their escape attempt in the village of Perbál (about 19 km from Budapest). Only a few men of the 'Billnitzer' Group managed to reach the German lines, while all other comrades perished or were captured.

Of the men defending the Budapest Fortress, only about 600-700 Germans and a few dozen Hungarians managed to escape the Soviet encirclement, reaching the coveted German lines in the direction of Vienna in small groups.

The siege of Budapest officially ended on 14 February 1945, when the Soviets managed to overwhelm the last remaining German-Hungarian defences, after the last defenders had largely surrendered on 13 February.

▲ Remains of the Zrínyi II of 1st Lieutenant Rácz of the 3rd Battery of the 1st Tank Battalion on a Budapest boulevard. The photograph was taken after the end of the armed conflict in Vérmező Park.

▼ Numerous Panzer-Faust tanks piled up in a trench in the defence of Budapest. In the absence of additional armour, the city's defenders used this devastating anti-tank weapon in large numbers.

▲ After the hell of the siege came the occupation of Budapest by Soviet troops. .

▼ Several armoured vehicles of the defenders abandoned after the fighting in a defenders' regrouping area in Budapest. Several Hetzer tanks and a Hummel, among others, can be seen.

1945: THE FINAL BATTLES

THE SWAN SONG OF THE HUNGARIAN ARMOURED FORCES

By the end of 1944, Hungary had split into two parts. The territories west of the Danube were controlled by the Germans and the Hungarian puppet government, while the remaining territories to the east were under Soviet control, which maintained the siege of the capital.

At the beginning of January 1945 a small battle group of the 2nd Armoured Division was subordinated to the Szent Lázsló Division, which participated in the Battle of the Garam River. The 3rd Tank Regiment had 3 38M Toldi and 2 Pz IV H. The 52nd Self-propelled Anti-Aircraft Artillery Battalion had 7 40M Nímrod. This was a very small number of troops. It seems that all of the still operational Zrinyi from the various tank battalions were transferred to the 20th and 24th Tank Battalions in January 1945. Despite this, their utilisation was considerably reduced due to the impossibility of keeping them operational under the conditions of continuous retreat that they had to endure.

On 1 January Tarczay was promoted to captain, after which he was given the mission to go with 40 of his men to Galánta (Galanta, Slovakia), where they picked up some new armoured vehicles for the 2nd Armoured Division on 8 January 1945. These were 27 Pz IV H (and according to some sources 2 Panther) which were to be used to give combat value to the 2nd Armoured Division. Similarly, some other unknown unit left several operational Zrínyi and Turán at the railway station in Stúrovo and near Bratislava (Slovakia) to receive new equipment from the Germans.

The 2nd Armoured Division with 15 Pz IV H and some additional vehicles participated in Operation Konrad I between 7 and 12 January 1945 in Székesfehérvár. On 7 January 1945 the Soviet attacks against the German 3rd Division and the 2nd Armoured Division were stopped in Csákvár.

On 16 January, the 2nd Armoured Division, already reinforced with 27 Pz IV H, plus 5 Nimrods, 1 Panther and a few other vehicles, prepared for the immediate fighting that awaited them. Captain Tarczay was placed in command of Pz IV H and deployed in the vicinity of the village of Bodajk together with the armoured units of the 1st Battalion.

On 24 January the 2nd Armoured Division, together with the 4th German Cavalry Brigade, supported the attack of the 1st Hussar Division on the Vértes Mountains. The Hungarians attacked at Csákvár with 11 Pz IV H and 4 Nimród. On 25 January 9 Hungarian and German tanks were destroyed by the Soviets.

The continuous fighting in retreat was bleeding the few remaining armoured units of the 2nd Armoured Division dry, prompting them in late February to try to form a defensive line near Székefehérvár and Zámoly, in the vicinity of Lakes Balaton and Velence. The 3rd/2nd Tank Battalion with 15 Pz IV H fought in Zámoly against the superior Soviet troops ready to take Hungary for good. The 2nd Armoured Division with 16 Pz IV H, 4 batteries and 4 motor battalions was subordinate to the 4th SS Armoured Corps.

Captain Tarczay, thanks to his important achievements in the subsequent battles in which he was involved, was able to enjoy a short and well-deserved period of rest, during which

▲ Top view of a Nimród, showing the open cockpit.

▲ Two Hungarian Pz IV H waiting in a concentration zone. Note the German insignia instead of the Hungarian one, a relatively frequent occurrence from 1944 onwards.

he married, and finally received the Hence Vitéz decoration on 15 March. On 16 March, the 3rd Ukrainian Front launched a powerful offensive against the Transdanubia, which enabled it to conquer the town of Csákberény and target the city of Vienna. In this advance, it was. Without further ado, on 17 March 1945 Tarczay returned to his unit and again took part in the fighting in command of 4 Pz IV H near the village of Söréd (three more Pz IV H were positioned at the Csókakö road junction). From there they did not have to move far, as the enemy was only a few kilometres away. Tarczay and his men took up a position on the road between Söréd and Csákberény, where they tried to stop the Soviet advance, but could not prevent the Soviets from encircling Söréd with infantry and armoured vehicles. On 18 March, around 20 Soviet Sherman tanks were sent against the town of Söréd in an attempt to break the Hungarian resistance, advancing along the road where Pz IV H from Tarczay was located. In this outnumbered Hungarian engagement (only 3 Pz IV H were involved), Tarczay and his men managed to destroy 2 Shermans, 2 trucks, 3 mortars and a Soviet infantry company.

The retreat was ordered by the Germans, but the complicated situation prevented them from retreating with their own forces, having to abandon them due to the extensive damage they suffered in combat, but not before they were finally destroyed. In their subsequent escape on foot through the swampy terrain west of Söréd, they were pursued by Russian troops who tried to annihilate them with small arms and mortar fire. During the escape, Captain Tarczay was severely wounded in the knee, causing severe bleeding, which, in the face of the imminent danger of being pursued by Soviet pursuers, they were unable to stop.

Bleeding to death and unable to be transported, Tarczay went into a state of shock and eventually died shortly after his despondent men abandoned him in this hellish escape. The Hungarian national hero and armoured ace was officially declared dead on 18 March 1945 after having destroyed more than 15 enemy tanks and at least a dozen anti-tank guns in the course of the fighting at the controls of various tanks such as the Turán 75, the Tiger, the Panther and the later Pz IV H.

In all the fighting around Söréd, the Hungarians lost 21 tanks and 70 trucks destroyed, while at least 35 armoured vehicles and 70 trucks were captured.

Despite the critical situation, some Hungarian armoured units still had a good number of vehicles. Thus, part of the 25th Tank Battalion, which was still fighting, had about 38 tanks (mainly Hetzer) at its disposal on 15 March 1945, although only six were operational.

▲ A Nimród column parades through a village with cannons at full height.

BUDAPEST RESCUE ATTEMPT

On 24 December 1944, Adolf Hitler, despite opposition from a large part of his General Staff, ordered SS Obergruppenführer Herbert Gille to prepare his powerful 4th SS Panzer Corps, which was recovering in the Warsaw area, to be sent to Hungary to participate in the attempt to liberate Budapest. To this end, Operation Konrad was launched in January 1945 in three phases, Konrad I, Konrad II and Konrad III.

The first phase or 'Konrad I' began on 1 January 1945 (and ended on 7 January). The 4th SS-Panzerkorps with its leading units (3rd SS Panzer Division 'Totenkopf' and 5th SS Panzer Division 'Viking') started from their positions in Táta (north of the capital) with the aim of breaking the encirclement of Budapest. Their attack was not preceded by artillery preparation to surprise the Soviets of the 4th Guard Army. Despite the initial blow, several Soviet units were dispatched within two days and managed to stop the German advance near Bicske, less than 20 kilometres from the capital. On 7 January the 'Esztergom-Bánhida' line was reached, but the Germans were finally stopped by the strong resistance put up by the Soviets.

After the initial failure, the second phase or "Konrad II" began on 7 January, with the aim of renewing the attack with the IV.SS-Panzerkorps from the town of Esztergom following the original plan, while the Breit Group attacked in the direction of Bicske from the southwest. These two forces would later join forces to begin the attack on the Budapest airport area. Again the attack was a fiasco due to the powerful defence put up by the Russians against the Germans, after an advance of no more than 6-7 kilometres.

▲ Two Turán II captured by the Soviets while being prepared for transport.

The third phase, or 'Konrad III', was prepared more thoroughly and with a larger number of troops. In addition, intelligence measures were taken to confuse the Soviets, such as sending the IV Corps to Győr and immediately moving it to Veszprém, where several units were gathering. Between the 17th and 18th, the offensive led by the IV SS-Panzerkorps and III Panzerkorps began, starting from the positions between Lakes Balaton and Velencei. The German advance broke through the first Soviet lines and, after reaching the Danube at Dunaújváros (today Dunapentele), turned north towards Budapest. Once again, strong Soviet resistance prevented them from reaching their final objective and they only managed to get within 20 kilometres of the capital. As part of these operations, the SS Ney (Hungarian) Regiment collaborated with the German armoured forces to capture the town of Székesfehérvár on 23 January. For their part, the besieged troops in Budapest asked permission to try to contact the units trying to rescue them, but they were not allowed to do so. After brutal attrition and without being able to make further progress, the attack was stopped on 28 January and the troops withdrew.

During the fighting north of the Hungarian capital between 1 January and 16 February 1945, what remained of the Hungarian 1st Army was practically annihilated. For their part, the few armoured troops the Hungarians still had available made few movements. It is known that the 20th Tank Assault Battalion with 16 Hetzers was subordinated to the 25th Infantry Division in February 1945.

▲ Several German armoured vehicles abandoned after being destroyed or disabled during the fighting. Although the battle for Budapest was not a battle in which armoured vehicles played the main role, they served as support for both attackers and defenders.

THE LAKE BALATON OFFENSIVE

The last major attempt to stop the Soviet advance in Hungary was called Operation Spring Awakening (unternehmen Frühlingserwachen) and is known as the Lake Balaton Offensive. Adolf Hitler, despite multiple setbacks on all fronts and the need for troops elsewhere, decided that Hungary would see a new offensive by his troops. The intention was to protect the south of the Reich and to recapture the Magyar oil areas, already in Soviet hands. The attack was to take place between Lakes Balaton and Velencei, stopping the advance of Tolbukhin's 3rd Ukrainian Front. After finishing them off, the next goal was to reach the Danube and from there attack Malinovsky's 2nd Ukrainian Front (which had just taken the Budapest Fortress three weeks earlier). Thanks to this second attack, the Hungarian capital would be recaptured. The Axis troops would then head north towards Berlin to prevent its capture and wipe out Zhukov and Koniev's troops. Although Hitler's objectives were extremely high, any positive outcome would have been attractive, as after the fall of Budapest and the failure of Operation Konrad, a blow on the Hungarian front was vital.

Among the Axis troops, the exhausted troops of Otto Wöhler's Army Group South (to which the Hungarian Third Army was attached) were assisted by the 6th SS Panzer Army, fresh from defeat in the Battle of the Bulge on the Western Front.

The main members of the Axis force were:

- The 6th Panzer SS Army: under the command of General Josef 'Sepp' Dietrich had to bear the brunt of the attack.
- 2nd Panzer Army: under the command of General Maximilian de Angelis, which would support the 6th Panzer SS Army south of Lake Balaton.
- 6th Army: under General Hermann Balck.
- Hungarian Third Army: under the command of General József Heszlényi, which had to support the Germans from the north of the offensive in a markedly secondary role, burdened even more by the absence of armoured equipment. It should also be mentioned that in the same theatre of operations remained the 20th Hungarian Tank Assault Battalion under the command of József Henkey-Hőnig, equipped with Hetzer tanks, which would practically represent the swan song of the Hungarian armoured forces in the Second World War.

In February 1945, the 20th High As Tank Battalion was reorganised into three batteries, but with a total of 15 assault tanks. The Battalion was assigned to the 25th Infantry Division towards the end of February, with which it is said to have fought with 8 Hetzers (two batteries) in support of an infantry attack against the Soviet 299th Rifle Division in the Balatonbozsok-Alsótekeres area near Lake Balaton.

By the end of February, the reinforcement of the 3rd Ukrainian Front after the fighting for the capital was complete. This included the Bulgarian 1st Army and many other units that would try to wipe out the much weakened Axis units in the western part of the country.

6 March 1945, between one and nine o'clock in the morning, was the date and time slot chosen to begin the attack on the positions of the 3rd Ukrainian Front. Although all information about the offensive was kept completely secret, the Soviets were aware of it and had prepared for it.

During the first two days, the attack was concentrated in the direction of Seregélyes, because it was thought that it would be easier to advance. But on 8 March, the attack had to be interrupted because the Soviets regrouped after the arrival of reinforcements.

On 8 March, 15 Hetzers of the 20th Hungarian Assault Tank Battalion and other troops fought alongside the remnants of the 4th German Cavalry Division and the 25th Hungarian Reconnaissance Battalion near Lake Balaton. Between 9 and 11 March the Hungarian 25th Infantry Division recaptured Enying with the support of the Hetzer Battalion. The 26th Infantry Regiment, supported by 15 Hetzers of the 20th Assault Tank Battalion, managed to break through the Russian lines of the 93rd Rifle Division at Siófok on 13 March 1945, but was repulsed, losing six Hetzers.

After several days of intense fighting in the cold Hungarian countryside, the Germans reached a level of attrition they could not afford (the effort was such that by 14 March they had suffered 30% casualties and 50-60% material losses). On the 15th, therefore, the 6th SS Panzer Army was ordered to stop the offensive and deploy on the defensive. The 'spring awakening' had ended 10 days after it began and the Soviets had only recovered a small portion of territory (between 30 and 35 kilometres), in exchange for the irreplaceable loss of many of their soldiers and much of their remaining armoured fleet. A small subunit of the 20th Hungarian Tank Assault with eight Hetzers participated in supporting the 23rd and 25th Infantry Regiments in an attack against the Soviet 299th Rifle Division in the Balatonboszok-Alsótekeres area.

Exhausted and unable to receive reinforcements, the territorial gains of the offensive were lost in only four days, as on 19 March the Soviets had returned to their front lines prior to Operation Spring Awakening. On 21 March, the 20th Magyar Assault Tank Battalion was withdrawn from the front line with thirteen Hetzers still operating.

▲ Famous photograph of a destroyed Hungarian Hetzer with the inscription Mókus (red squirrel) on the front. This vehicle, on which Soviet identification numbers are visible, was put out of action around March 1945 in western Hungary.

This last attempt by Hitler to take control of the situation on the Hungarian front resulted in easily recoverable losses for the Soviets, about 33,000 men (dead and wounded), more than 150 armoured vehicles and about 500 anti-tank guns. But for the Germans and Hungarians, the retreat into Reich territory began, leaving Hungary behind. The last combat operations on Hungarian soil took place around 4 April 1945 as part of the offensive on Vienna, so the last battles of the Hungarian armoured troops did not take place in the homeland, which had already been conquered by the Soviets (although many Hungarian troops surrendered in Hungarian territory and others in the territory of the former Czechoslovakia). While this disbandment was taking place, Szálasi went into exile in Germany with some of his supporters, giving up the battle at home for good.

THE FINAL FIGHTS

The next Axis defensive action in this theatre of operations was to focus on protecting the Hungarian north-west, Austrian territory and its capital. In reality, the German-Hungarian troops still had three defensive lines ready behind the Margit Line. The first ran from Általér towards Vértes and through the south-western foothills of the Bakony Forest to Lake Balaton. The second line followed the course of the Vág and Rába rivers, while the third line started from the south-western foothills of the Lesser Carpathians and ran along the Hungarian border. The problem, however, was the same as with the other Magyar defence lines, which in some areas were neither continuous nor fully consolidated, consisting in some cases of only a few interconnected fortifications.

The objective of the 3rd Ukrainian Front was to break through the German-Hungarian defences by directing its main attack in the direction of Székesfehérvár and Veszprém, thus pinning down the main defensive units.

After completing the taking of Hungary, the next step was to reach the Vienna area, now inside the Reich, at the beginning of April.

▲ Some newly produced Nimród rest in a military depot before being sent to the destination unit.

However, on 20 March Tolbukhin's 26th and 27th Armies were sent in the direction of Székesfehérvár, causing a general retreat of the defenders who, although they could not be encircled, abandoned their positions at Veszprém and Székesfehérvár on 23 March. Only two days later, the 3rd Ukrainian Front and the forces of the 2nd Ukrainian Front south of the Danube managed to break through the last defences in Magyar territory, causing the Germans and Hungarians to generally disband. Many of the individual Hungarian soldiers laid down their arms and tried to return home after stripping themselves of their uniforms, already occupied by the Soviets, in some cases to be recruited by the Soviets for the formation of pro-Soviet Hungarian troops such as the 5th Magyar Infantry Division (only one unit, the 24th Infantry Division, largely deserted).

On 21 March, meanwhile, the last operational Zrínyi of the 24th Tank Battalion surrendered in Bratislava (Slovakia), as did a handful of surviving Turán I. The retreat was northwards, with the fall of the city of Győr (the second largest city in Hungary) on 28 March. The retreat was northwards, with the fall of the city of Győr (Hungary's second largest city) on 28 March. On the 29th Szálasi and his government left Magyar territory for Austria. However, some Axis forces remained on Hungarian territory and the fighting continued at least until 12 April 1945. At that point, when all of Hungary was occupied by the Soviets, there were still three small areas where the Hungarians continued to fight: the remnants of the 1st Army were in Slovakia (where they had been pushed), to continue their retreat to Bohemia, where they would eventually surrender to the Soviets; the 3rd Army (which contained what was once the 2nd Armoured Division) was in Austria along the north bank of the Danube, where it would be captured by the Western Allies; Finally, a set of units, notably the 'Szent László', was forced to return from northern Croatia (where it was fighting Tito's partisans, who took advantage of the retreat to decimate the Magyars) to Austria, where it surrendered to the British. Interestingly, the men of the 'Szent László' were allowed by the British to continue arming themselves as a measure against Tito's communist troops.

But this retreat of the Germans and Hungarians had to take place under very difficult weather conditions, with snow and mud that did not make the task any easier. This situation was taken advantage of by the Soviet advances and partisan troops (especially those in Czech territory) who decimated the Axis soldiers, as happened to the remnants of the 1st Hungarian Armoured Division and the 20th Tank Battalion. These harassments and the lack of fuel meant that during the march to the north of the country, some of the few Hungarian armoured vehicles were abandoned, still in fighting condition, as they tried to reach the German Reich fleeing the Soviets. Examples are the armoured vehicles abandoned at Zaim (Znojmo) on the Czech-Austrian border or at the Budafok-Háros railway station, which became Soviet spoils of war.

As a human result of the final defeat, more than half a million Hungarians (an estimated 419,000 to 600,000) were deported to labour camps in Siberia, where about 40 per cent of them died (at least 200,000 did not return home). The survivors returned home between 1953 and 1956. As a material result, Hungary regained practically the same territories it had in 1938, with the exception of a small territorial loss on the border with Czechoslovakia. All the annexations that had taken place between 1938 and 1941 and all hopes of rebuilding a Greater Hungary had been definitively eliminated.

ANNEXES

ANNEX 1: ARMOURED VEHICLES OF THE HUNGARIAN ARMY

The Hungarian armoured forces, as we have seen in the text, were unable to face the powerful Soviet enemy on equal terms during all phases of the world war. However, the Hungarian government's commendable attempt to build an armoured force based on domestic production is noteworthy. Although the course of the war prevented the development of the last Hungarian projects, it is quite likely that had they seen active service, they would have been much more on par with their Soviet adversaries. Hungarian necessity eventually allowed Germany to deliver various types of armoured vehicles to Hungary, including the mighty Tiger and Panther, albeit in such small numbers that they provided no strategic effectiveness.

In this section we will briefly review the most significant armoured vehicles of different characteristics that, to a greater or lesser extent, were part of the Hungarian army during the Second World War, with a focus on those of Hungarian manufacture.

TANKS OF FOREIGN ORIGIN

1) Panzer I

One example was delivered to the Hungarians in 1937 for testing. Later, in 1942, the Honved received from Germany eight examples of the Pz I Ausf. F that were used for training the crews of the 1st Armoured Division. Perhaps another example of an earlier model was received in the same year. Evidently, these vehicles could never be used as frontline armoured vehicles due to their obsolescence early in the conflict.

2) Renault R-35

The Magyars used three units supplied by Germany. These tanks with a 37 mm cannon were part of the spoils of war obtained in Poland and were to be used in the second line. Despite their excellent armour, they were under-armoured and it was almost suicidal to use them in the front line.

3) M 3 Stuart

Several examples of this American model with 37 mm cannon were captured by the Soviets and used as tractors. They arrived in the USSR thanks to the Lend-Lease law in force between 1941 and 1945.

4) T-11 (LT vz. 35)

Two units of this tank with a 37 mm cannon were captured during the fighting between Hungary and Czechoslovakia (March 39). They were used for training purposes.

5) T-38 (LT vz. 38 or Pz 38)

Hungary received 108 tanks of this model with 37 mm cannon from Germany. This was the country's first attempt to purchase modern armoured equipment from abroad. The main problem was that by the time they were received (in 1942) they were already obsolete, so they would prove to be little capable of being a serious opponent for the Soviet armoured vehicles they would face, being poorly armed and poorly armoured.

6) Somua S-35

Only two examples of this French tank with 47 mm cannon entered the Hungarian arsenal. Both vehicles were used for anti-partisan activity in Ukraine, as they were of little use against Soviet tanks.

7) Pz IIIM

Hungary received 20 units of this German 50 mm model. They were divided equally between the 1st and 2nd Armoured Divisions. The small number of units received did not allow Hungary to tip the balance on the side of the Soviets.

8) Pz IV F1

It was the first tank the Hungarians possessed capable of facing Soviet opponents on equal terms. With its short 75 mm KwK 37 L/24 cannon, the Germans considered it a medium tank, while the Hungarians classified it as a heavy tank.

9) Pz IV F2

It was the logical evolution of the F1 model, with the replacement of the main gun with the 75 mm KwK 40 L/43 long gun, which improved its anti-tank capability. About 10 examples of this model were integrated into the 1st Armoured Division in 1942.

10) Pz IV H

As wartime events unfolded, Germany had to strengthen the armoured capacity of its allies and in 1944 the Hungarians received 72 tanks. These tanks were equipped with the powerful 75 mm KwK 40 L/48 anti-tank gun, which, together with the 80 mm frontal protection, made the Pz IV H the heart of Hungarian armoured power.

According to Bernád, the Pz IVs received by the Hungarians between May and August 1944 (32 in number) were of the Pz IVG model; from September 1944 the models received were Pz IVH. As a curiosity, it is worth mentioning that the last delivery of these tanks to the Hungarians took place in March 1945, when several examples were delivered.

11) Pz V A Panther

Fortunately, between 10 and 12 units of this magnificent armour arrived in Hungary. Their arrival was actually fortuitous, as their original destination was Romania, but the change of deployment in 1944 diverted them to Hungary, where they served with great efficiency. Armed with the 75 mm KwK 42/L70 cannon and two 7.92 mm MG 34 machine guns, it was, after the Tiger, the most powerful Hungarian tank.

12) Pz VI Tiger I

One of the jewels of the German armament industry and of exclusive use to its armies was also part of the Hungarian arsenal. Under other circumstances, Germany would not have supplied these armoured vehicles, but the need to somehow reinforce the weak armoured units of the Hungarian ally led it to make this decision.

Ten Tiger I units of sPzAbt.503 or sPzAbt.509 were delivered in July 1944 to the Hungarians by rail. Another three units were delivered by the Germans as gifts.

These tanks were used in defensive battles against the Soviets, in which they proved their valour. By the end of July 1944, they had already suffered seven losses in these bloody battles, but mainly due to the lack of fuel, which forced them to abandon the tanks. To their credit, they had managed to destroy at least 22 Soviet tanks during this period.

13) T-34/76
There is a photograph showing a T-34/76 tank of Soviet origin with stripes in Hungarian colours. It is a captured vehicle that was occasionally used by Hungarian units in small numbers. There are also sources that mention the T-34/85 model among those captured by Hungary.

14) Hotchkiss H-35/H-39
Some examples of this French-made tank were later used by the Hungarian army. They came from Germany, which had taken them as war booty after the conquest of France. Their poor combat capability relegated them to anti-partisan tasks.

15) Other
During the invasion of the USSR, some minor Soviet armoured vehicles fell into Hungarian hands, fit for use. Their subsequent use was usually not for combat, but as tractors. These included the more than six BT-7 and T-26 captured in 1941-1942. Also in the same period, between four and six BA-6s were obtained as spoils of war.

Comparison table of main battle tanks of foreign origin:

	ORIGIN	CREW MEMBERS	WEIGHT (tonnes)	MAIN WEAPON	SPEED Km/h	MAIN BLINDNESS (mm)
Pcs 38	CZECHOSLOVAKIA		10.5	37 mm	42	50
Pz IIIM	GERMANY	5	21.1	50 mm	40	70
Pz IV F1	GERMANY	5	22.3	75 mm	42	80
Pz IV F2	GERMANY	5	23.6	75 mm	40	80
Pz IV H	GERMANY	5	26	75 mm		80
PZ V A	GERMANY	5	44.8	75 mm	55	110
Pz VI	GERMANY	5	56.9	88 mm	45	100

HUNGARIAN-MADE TANKS

1) Straussler V4 light tank
Only a prototype of this tank with a 23 mm cannon was built and the idea of mass production was abandoned in 1937. Despite domestic production (Manfred Weiss), its rival and replacement was to be a new tank based on the Swedish Landsverk L-60, called the Toldi.

2) Toldi light tank (models 38M, 41M, 42M and 43M)
In 1937, the Hungarian government held a competition between three light tank models to choose the one that would form the core of its armoured forces and be produced in Hungarian factories. The competitors were the Straussler, the German Pz I and the Swedish Landsverk L-60. The winner was the latter, partly due to its advanced development for the time and its excellent characteristics.

Once chosen, the Hungarians requested a number of modifications to the original model to make it more suitable for their needs. These included ventilation, suspension, aiming system and transmission, but the most important was the adoption of the Solothurn 36M 20mm anti-tank gun, accompanied by an 8mm coaxial machine gun (34/37 AM) and an R-5 radio. The cannon had a range of about 2,000 metres and had 208 projectiles with an exit velocity of 735 mm. The cannon had a range of about 2,000 metres and had 208 projectiles with an exit velocity of 735 m/sec. The rate of fire was 30-35 rounds per minute and the penetration capacity was 20 mm at 100 metres and 16 mm at 500 m at 30°.

Besides the limited firepower, another major handicap was the tank's limited armour, which was more suited to infantry attacks than other armoured vehicles.

The new tank was named 38M Toldi I (after the 14th century Hungarian warrior Miklos Toldi) and its production under licence was ordered from the MÁVAG and Ganz factories. But the first units did not leave the factories until much later, the first two units in February 1940, while the first order for 20 units from the Hungarian Ministry of Defence did not come until June 1940.

The 38M Toldi I, although produced in Hungary, still had several parts that had to be procured from Sweden and Germany; nevertheless, it achieved a total production of 80 units between 1940 and 1941.

After the 38M and due to the numerous modifications that the Hungarians made to the new tanks, the next 110 examples produced between 1941 and 1942 (68 by Ganz and 42 by MÁVAG) received the designation 41M Toldi II. These examples had some improvements over the previous model, such as the R-5/a radio, and above all, every single part was produced in Hungary.

After all the modifications made over the months, it was difficult to distinguish a Todi I from a Toldi II, except for the differently made antenna.

The Toldi's mediocre combat performance was improved by increasing firepower and armour (this improvement could not be carried out adequately because the inability of the engine to cope with the increase in weight was assessed). Thus in 1943 appeared the new 42M Toldi IIa model, which switched from a 20 mm cannon to a 40 mm cannon (the 37/42M MÁVAG, which was a licence for the 40 mm Bofors), and although the improvement was evident, it was still completely insufficient to compete with Soviet rivals. In fact, 80 Toldi IIs were used for this new model, rearmed with the new cannon and other less important modifications. Another significant modification was the replacement of the machine gun with the Gebauer 34/40AM.

The new artillery piece required some modifications to the Toldi II's turret, leaving the tank with a capacity of 55 40 mm shells. Again, this was one of the tank's Achilles heels, as its penetration capacity was only 30 mm at 1000 m at an angle of 30° and 64 mm at 100 m at the same angle. Its characteristics included a bullet exit velocity of 800 m/s and the ability to fire 16 bullets in one minute.

The speed achieved by a Toldi with its 155-160 hp engine, subject to small variations depending on the model, was 47-50 km/h on the road; with a range of 190 to 220 km.

As already mentioned, the vehicle's other weak point was its armour, which was always insufficient to cope with the medium and large calibre parts used by the Soviets (remember that the front end was only 35 mm thick). In spite of attempts at improvement, such as the addition of 5-8 mm side skirts (köténylemez in Hungarian), in the end these were only small touches that did not significantly increase the survival of the vehicle in combat.

The obsolescence of the Toldi IIa, despite the modifications, was aggravated by the slowness with which these took place. In fact, although the conversion began in early 1943, it was not completed until 1944.

The Hungarian Army demanded a solution that could definitively take the Toldi to a higher combat level, using it exclusively as an armoured reconnaissance vehicle. In response to this request, Hungarian industry designed a further improvement of the vehicle, called the Toldi III 43M, in which the armour and ammunition capacity were enhanced. However, the war situation further limited Hungarian industrial capacity and, together with the Hungarian government's decision to promote other projects, meant that only 12 examples of the new Toldi could be put into service. The Ganz company was commissioned to redesign it with a 35 mm front armour (both on the hull and turret), a 25 mm side armour on the turret and a 20 mm side armour on the hull. The cannon calibre remained the same as the Toldi IIa, although the turret was increased in size.

In any case, the Toldi only proved useful in reconnaissance, liaison or security roles in the rear, as they were easy prey to enemy fire and front-line damage; for this reason, after 1941, the Toldi in armoured formations were only used as reconnaissance vehicles.

Total production of the Toldi in its various models reached 202 units, which had to change its role within the Hungarian armoured forces from a main battle tank to a simple armoured reconnaissance vehicle.

As with many tanks, a couple of variants were developed from its chassis to give a second life to obsolete vehicles.

The first of these variants originated from 9 Toldi I modified to provide frontline medical assistance (in this case retaining the functional cannon but with less ammunition). These vehicles were modified in 1942 and named 43M Toldi Egészségügyi (doctors). According to Becze, 4 vehicles were converted in 1942 and 9 between 1943 and 1944. Characteristically, they were equipped to carry two stretchers and had enlarged doors for easy access. They were incorporated into the 2nd Army, where they operated on the front line.

Continuing with the history of the Toldi tank, it is necessary to refer to two evolutions of the tank that, despite initial interest, did not lead to their mass production: the Toldi PaK 40 L/48 and the Toldi with 44M Buzogányvető rocket launcher.

Toldi PaK 40 L/48

Having had several German Marders on loan between 1942 and 1943, which had more than proved their worth, one of these was sent to the Hungarian Institute of Military Technology to be tested and studied in detail before being returned. Based on this knowledge, the aim was to build a 'Hungarian Marder', a fighter based on the Toldi's chassis, only with an open structure housing a non-rotating German PaK 40 75 mm L/48 cannon. The prototype was developed by Ganz in the autumn of 1943 from a Toldi I under repair.

This replacement for the Marder had several disadvantages that made it refuse mass production, such as: the poor armour, resistant only to rifle fire, the weakness of the Toldi I's shock-absorption system, the excessive height and narrow width, which made it unstable, and above all the fact that the Hungarian industry had focused on the Turán family and the Zrínyi, which meant that it could not afford any other indigenous vehicles.

▲ A Toldi IIAK with side skirts that increased its durability in combat missions, although it was always inferior to Soviet anti-tank guns.

Toldi with rocket launcher 44M Buzogányvető

In a desperate attempt to increase the power of the Hungarian artillery, Hungarian industry had worked on the design of a rocket similar to those used by the Germans. This rocket was named 44M Buzogányvető (after the German occupation of Hungary on 16 October 1944, it would be renamed 'Szálasi-röppentyű', after the 'Szálasi flyer' named after the leader of the Arrow Cross party).

Two types of this 100 mm rocket launcher were developed: an anti-tank rocket (HEAT: high explosive anti-tank) with the nickname Buzogány (mace); and a second anti-personnel model called Zápor (rain).

The first prototype of the Buzogány was produced and tested in the spring of 1944. It carried an explosive warhead weighing about 4 kg and could penetrate 300 mm of armour or concrete, making it capable of attacking any Soviet tank at a distance of 500 to 1,200 metres. The first option was to use a three-legged stand, but this did not allow it to be moved with agility. Later, weapons captured from the Soviets, such as the wheeled bases of the Soviet Maxim machine guns or the SG-43 Goryunov, were used as mounts. This was clearly an improvement, but the aim was to give this new weapon maximum capability.

The next step was the use of vehicles to support the rocket launcher: one possibility was the Krupp Protze truck, to which the Opel Blitz or the Hungarian Rába Botond was to be added.

About 600-700 of these rocket launchers were produced by WM industries before the surrender to the Soviets. Most of them were used for the defence of the Hungarian capital.

After studying the possibilities of support vehicles for rocket launchers, two armoured vehicles were evaluated: the Toldi and the Nimród.

▲ The only known image of the Hungarian 'Marder'. Despite its non-rotating 75 mm PaK 40 L/48 cannon, being based on a Toldi I, it was poorly armoured.

At least one Toldi II was prepared with a rocket mount. Fortunately, a photograph exists which, although not of good quality and not taken at a good angle, gives an idea of what it might have looked like. As for the Nimród, according to one source (Béla Toronyi, who worked as a mechanic where these modifications were carried out) in 1944 at least 2-3 Nimród chassis were modified to support the rocket launcher. According to the same source, two vehicles with the Buzogányvető incorporated took part in one battle each, both destroyed during combat.

3) 40/43M Turan
This Hungarian-built tank was based on a Czechoslovakian prototype called the T-21 (former Skoda S-IIc). After the invasion of Czechoslovakia, this prototype (as well as many others) was studied by the Germans, who eventually scrapped it for their own use.
Towards the end of May 1940, Germany authorised licensed production of the T-21 in Hungary. In June of the same year, a prototype of the T-21 was sent by train to Hungary with the Czech crew and mechanics, to be tested at the Hajmáské test field.
The Hungarian engineers made a number of changes to the original model, such as replacing the original 47 mm cannon with a 40 mm cannon (specifically a 40 mm L/45 with a muzzle velocity of 800 m/s and a rate of fire of 16 rounds per minute; it was a variant of the standard Hungarian anti-tank cannon and also shared ammunition with the Bofors anti-aircraft cannon, also in the Hungarian arsenal). The projectile could penetrate 64 mm of armour (at 30° inclination) at 100 metres and 30 mm at 1000 metres at the same inclination. Another noteworthy modification was the replacement of the ZB-37 machine guns with 8 mm Gebauer machine guns.

The Turán I entered service on 28 November 1941 and was officially named 40.M Turán közepes harckocsi (medium tank) and colloquially Turán I or Turán 40. The name Turán was given in homage to the Hungarian ancestral homeland in Central Asia.

The first prototype of the Turan was built by Manfred Weiss on 8 July 1941. Due to suspension and transmission problems, series production was delayed until early 1942. Long before it could enter combat, the Turan was completely obsolete.

Of the total production of the Turan I, 20 examples were modified into a command tank (Turan I P.K.) with an additional radio to replace part of the ammunition.

As a result of the Hungarian army's Huba modernisation programme, the total production of 40M Turán (Turán I) tanks reached 235 (285 according to Németh), produced by Weiss Manfréd (70), Magyar Waggonyár (70), MÁVAG (50) and Ganz (45). As a curiosity, the Turán pieces from the various manufacturers were not exactly the same.

In February 1943, all Turán had to be sent to factories in Hungary for repairs, which lasted several months.

Even before the first Turan I arrived at the front, it was clear that both the armour and armament were totally inadequate to cope with most Soviet armoured vehicles. For this reason, the 41M Turan II appeared in May 1943 with a few improvements, most notably the replacement of the main part with a short 75 mm cannon developed by MÁVAG, which was clearly insufficient to put it on a par with Soviet tanks, as the low projectile speed was unable to pierce the frontal armour of a T-34 except at almost point-blank range. So the 75 mm (based on the 76.6 mm Böhler, recalibrated by Bofors) was not much more effective than the 40 mm of the Turan I.

The Turán II was also known as Turán 75 rövid (short), Nehéz Turán (heavy Turán) or simply T-75.

Some 139 Turán IIs were produced between 1943 and 1944 (according to Németh, 182-185 tanks were produced, including some Turán Is that were upgraded to Turán II level). After

▲ Another picture of the Turán command, of which only this prototype was produced in 1943.

the German occupation of Hungary on 19 March 1944, production slowed down and was limited exclusively to the production of spare parts (but not new vehicles) and was finally stopped in the summer of 1944 by German order, ending production shortly before the German invasion of Hungary.

Another development was the 43M Turán III, the main feature of which was the modified turret with the addition of a long 75 mm piece (a Hungarian copy of the German 7.5 cm Pak 40, called the 75 mm 43 M L/55), as well as more armour. As it was not possible to incorporate this piece into the same turret as the Turán I or II, it had to be redesigned, resulting not only in a wider and longer turret, but also a taller one, with the consequent problems of tank concealment. In February 1944, only one prototype of the Turán III was built, which represented the pinnacle of Hungarian tank evolution and, had it been mass-produced, would have been a serious rival to the Soviets.

The maximum armour on the front of the Turan was 50 mm, rising to 60 mm on later models. In the other parts of the tank, the armour varied from 8 to 25 mm in the horizontal parts and from 25 to 40 mm in the vertical parts. In any case, this was derisory protection against the 76.2 or 85 mm guns of the Soviets. Attempts were made to alleviate the problem by copying the Germans in the use of armoured skirts on the turret and flanks, with minimal success. In the case of the Turan III, the front armour would be 80 mm and the 8 mm side skirts would be standard.

Turán's most important conversion was that of Zrínyi, which will be discussed separately because of its importance.

A final variant of the Turan is the version with a dummy cannon, intended for use as a command vehicle.

4) 44M TAS

The 44M TAS medium tank (possibly named after a 9th century Magyar warrior) was the last attempt to solve the problem of the Hungarian tanks' inferiority to their German or Soviet counterparts once and for all. This time, partly based on the lessons learned from the evaluation of the German Panther tank, the aim was to produce an indigenous tank with adequate protection and armament, capable of destroying any enemy it might encounter. Although the Hungarian government's first attempt was to acquire the licence rights to the Panther, this possibility was rejected by the Germans. Later, a small number of Panthers were integrated into the Hungarian armoured forces after being diverted from their original destination of Romania (following the country's change of deployment).

The TAS carried a 75 mm cannon (the German KwK 42L/70) and two 8 mm machine guns and its frontal armour was about 100-120 mm thick. Its maximum speed on the road reached 48 km/h and its crew consisted of five men.

All in all, the TAS would have been a worthy rival to Soviet tanks, had it gone into series production. But only a prototype was built in March 1944, without further production continuity, mainly due to the partial destruction of Weiss Industries after the American bombing raid on 27 July 1944. The subsequent conflict prevented further development.

Based on the TAS chassis, a tank destroyer design was developed, just like the Jagdpanther for the Panther.

Comparison table of the main Hungarian tanks:

	ORIGIN	CREW MEMBERS	WEIGHT (tonnes)	MAIN WEAPON	SPEED Km/h	MAIN BLINDNESS (mm)
Toldi I	HUNGARY		8.7	20 mm	50	
Toldi II	HUNGARY		8.7	20 mm	50	
Toldi IIa	HUNGARY		9.35	40 mm		
Toldi III	HUNGARY		9.45	40 mm	45	35
Turan I	HUNGARY	5	18.2	40 mm		50
Turan II	HUNGARY	5	19.2	75 mm	45	50
Turan III	HUNGARY	5		75 mm	40	80
TAS	HUNGARY	5		75 mm	48	120

SELF-PROPELLED GUNS OF FOREIGN MANUFACTURE

1) Marder II Ausf.A/B/C/F

This German tank fighter was based on the Pz II chassis (in its various A/B/C/F models). With its powerful 75 mm cannon, and despite the few units leased to Hungary by Germany, it proved to be one of the best anti-tank weapons the Magyars were able to deploy against the Soviets.

Its main defect was its poor 30 mm armour and the fact that it did not have a turret but an open cockpit.

Hungarian satisfaction with this vehicle prompted the development of the 'Hungarian Marder'.

According to Bernád, at least one copy of Marder III was delivered to the Magyars in October 1944.

2) StuG III Ausf.G

One of the most versatile assault cannons used by the Germans also entered the arsenal of the Magyars. Fifty units were delivered to Hungary (according to Károly Németh, the number would rise to 60, of which 20 were only temporarily controlled by the Magyars), which in 1944 allowed the 7th Assault Cannon Battalion of the 1st Hungarian Armoured Division to be equipped with 40 units, in addition to other units serving in the 2nd Armoured Division. The StuG III was equipped with a 75 mm StuK L/48 (Ausf.G) long gun and, although originally intended as an assault gun, at this point in the conflict it was mainly used as a tank destroyer, with great effectiveness. This was amply demonstrated when, together with the Zrínyi, they managed to destroy at least 67 Soviet tanks on 9 October 1944 with the loss of only 10 StuG IIIs during the Battle of Szentes.

3) Jagdpanzer 38(t) Hetzer

The German Reich had to strengthen the dying Hungarian armoured capacity by selling 130 examples of this versatile light tank destroyer between 1944 and 1945. With its 75 mm

L/48 cannon and 7.92 mm machine gun, it fought the last defensive battles in Hungary with great success, eventually being overwhelmed by Soviet troops. The number of these vehicles received by Hungary ranged from 75 to 150, used exclusively in the final stages of the war, where destruction and chaos reigned. The latter fact is the reason why there is little documentation of their use by the Magyars.

As a curiosity, the first units of this vehicle supplied by the Germans went to the 1st Cavalry Division in Poland in August 1944.

The last Hetzers received by the Magyars were received in January 1945, when 25 (and possibly 16 more) were handed over by the Germans in view of the turn of events in Magyar territory.

Comparative table of the main German assault tanks:

	ORIGIN	CREW MEMBERS	WEIGHT (tonnes)	MAIN WEAPON	SPEED Km/h	MAIN BLINDNESS (mm)
Marder II	GERMANY		10.8	75 mm	40	35
StuG III	GERMANY		23.9	75 mm	40	80
Hetzer	GERMANY			75 mm	42	

HUNGARIAN-MADE SELF-PROPELLED CANNONS

1) 40/43M Zrínyi II

This development of the Turán tank originated from the Hungarian industry's attempt to find a suitable rival to the Soviets with a lower degree of difficulty in its manufacture. Basically, the spirit of the German Sturmgeschutz III was copied and developed from the Pz III tank. As with the StuG III, the Hungarian idea was to develop two variants: one with an assault gun carrying a 105 mm howitzer and the other with a 75 mm anti-tank gun (Zrínyi II and Zrínyi I respectively); in both cases the chassis on which they would be mounted would be that of the Turán tank. The Zrínyi II was also called the Zrínyi 105 assault howitzer, while the Zrínyi I was called the Zrínyi 75 assault gun. The name Zrínyi is in honour of Nikolaus Graf Zrínyi, a national hero who died in the Battle of Szigetvár against the Turks in 1566.

The prototype version of the assault cannon was tested on 12 December 1942 and accepted for series production on 20 January 1943.

The Zrinyi II (40/43M Zrinyi II) reached 43 km/h on the road and carried a 105 mm howitzer (40/43M L/20.5), which was a tank version of the 105 mm 40M field howitzer. Despite its calibre, being a howitzer, the projectile had a low exit velocity (448 m/sec) which gave it some capability against armoured vehicles such as the T-34, but minimal against Stalin or ISU-152 heavy tanks and tank destroyers.

A final observation on the Zrínyi II concerns the type of projectile used. Initially, the characteristics of a short-barreled howitzer were far from ideal for dealing with enemy armour. But the Hungarian armament industry began working to remedy this situation, at least in part. The change from the HE 38/33M 105 mm projectile (which was a fragmentation grenade) to the HEAT 42M 105 mm projectile (anti-tank explosive) improved the effectiveness of the Zrínyi II, somewhat increasing its survivability on the battlefield (as it did not need such close distances from the enemy to fire).

The protective armament included an 8mm coaxial machine gun (34/40M).

Another armament option considered in Hungary was to equip the Zrínyi II with the 150 mm Nebelwerfer 41 rocket launcher. These would have performed a similar mission to the German Army's Nebelwerfer on the Opel Maultier, allowing for great movement and firepower. Even this armament option was not eventually developed.

In terms of passive protection, this tank had 75 mm frontal armour, 13 to 25 mm in the horizontal areas and 25 to 40 in the vertical areas; it was upgraded in the same way as the Turan, with side skirts (albeit with a mesh design that did not excessively increase the weight of the vehicle, similar to the German Von Thoma armour).

Initial production of the Zrinyi II was 40 examples in 1943, followed by a production order for 104. But the course of the war limited final production to around 60 vehicles (perhaps 66 if Ganz had managed to deliver another six between August and September 1944). According to Becze, 72 were produced in total, although it is difficult to verify this number. The cause was once again the Allied bombing of Manfred Industries in July 1944, which brought production to a complete halt after destroying most of the infrastructure.

2) 44M Zrínyi I

As for the 44M Zrínyi I fighter, it can only be said that it never got beyond the prototype stage, completed in February 1944. Production was set for June 1944 due to some mechanical problems with the prototype, but the bombed Manfred and Ganz factories were unable to even attempt production, which was therefore postponed until autumn 1944. In reality, no further progress was made and already by the autumn of 1944, traces of the only one built were lost. Had Hungary had the 44M Zrínyi I, this powerful tank destroyer would

▲ Picture of the only prototype Zrínyi I armed with a 75 mm gun at the military depot in Tüzérszertár. A Zrínyi II with a 105 mm howitzer can be seen behind.

undoubtedly have been a serious opponent for Soviet armoured vehicles and in some ways would have tipped the balance of the fighting in favour of the Hungarians.

3) Tas 44 M Röhamloveg (Tas assault rifle)

This destroyer was a design based on mounting a German KwK 43 L/71 88 mm gun in a casemate on the chassis of a Tas 44 M medium tank. It was in 1944, as the development of the Tas 44M tank progressed, that Hungarian engineers decided to develop a highly advanced destroyer. In its design, great attention was paid to its silhouette, which was very low, allowing it to remain undetected by enemies for longer. It would also become a valuable weapon in ambushes and defensive combats. In addition to the powerful main weapon, it possessed two defensive machine guns.

Weiss Manfréd was commissioned to produce the two prototypes ordered. However, although some components were produced, they never materialised for the same reasons as the Tas 44 M tank. In fact, according to recent studies, such as that of Károly Németh, there is no evidence that not the prototype, but even parts of the Tas tank were assembled.

HUNGARIAN-MADE TANKS

1) 39/40M Csaba

One of the first Hungarian-made armoured vehicles to be widely used in the Honved was the Csaba tank. In 1935, engineer Michael Straussler, with the support of Manfred Weiss, developed a 4 x 4 armoured reconnaissance vehicle with a double driving position (front and rear). After several trials in which the Csaba competed with other foreign-made models, the Hungarian army gave the go-ahead for series production.

The official designation was 39 M Csaba (named after the son of Attila the Hun) and was assigned to Hungarian reconnaissance units.

▲ Hungarian soldiers looked with curiosity at the Polish tanks that had taken refuge in Hungary from the Germans. These tanks were a Polish development of the British Carden-Lloyd tank. The Hungarians used 20 ex-Polish units: 9 TK-3, 7 TKS and 4 TKS.

The main armament consisted of the 20mm Solothurn 36M cannon and an 8mm machine gun, both positioned in a central turret. A second machine gun was positioned in the aft hatch for anti-aircraft protection, with the possibility of being used by the crew for reconnaissance on foot.

In 1939, 61 vehicles were ordered, followed by a further 20 in 1940, although the latter were designated 40M Csaba as they were built as a command version. The latter model did not have a cannon, so the turret was smaller, but had more powerful radio equipment. Final production between 1939 and 1944 reached 145 vehicles, 105 39M and 40 40M.

Its reconnaissance performance was excellent, although it paid dearly for the weakness of its armour. By the end of 1941, over 90 per cent of the vehicles produced had been destroyed. From then on, its combat use was reduced and it was used in small numbers by various units.

FOREIGN-MADE TANKS

1) 35M Ansaldo

This Italian tank, developed in 1935 by FIAT and popularly known as Ansaldo, was armed with two 8 mm machine guns. About 120 examples served under the Hungarian flag (152 according to Becze). Despite the expectations placed on their use, it soon became clear that their design was obsolete and that they were extremely vulnerable in combat. This meant that they had to be used for secondary tasks to safeguard them. As a curiosity, one of the examples received was prepared as a flamethrower vehicle.

2) TKS

This tank was a Polish development of the British Carden-Lloyd tank. The Hungarians used 20 ex-Polish examples: 9 TK-3, 7 TKS and 4 TKS. Its main use was for training or as a companion to the Ansaldo.

3) T-27

The T-27 was a Soviet version of the British Carden-Loyd tank, armed with a 7.62 mm DT or 12.7 mm DsHK machine gun. Some examples (more than 10) were put into service with the Hungarian Army as artillery tractors or for training purposes after being captured by the Soviets on the Eastern Front during the invasion of the USSR.

OTHER ARMOURED VEHICLES OF HUNGARIAN MANUFACTURE

1) Armoured anti-aircraft vehicle 40M Nimród

The Hungarian army, after the fighting for the annexation of part of Slovakia, experienced the importance of adequate anti-aircraft protection. Moreover, in view of the creation of a nascent rapid armoured force, this anti-aircraft protection could not only be static, but a vehicle had to be created that could follow the mobile units with adequate speed. The result of these demands was the Nimród, although the first vehicle chosen to carry out this mission was the L-62 anti-aircraft vehicle of Swedish origin. Derived from the Landsverk

L-60 (produced under licence in Hungary as the 38M Toldi I), this vehicle could easily be integrated into the national production of armoured vehicles. After formalising the situation with the Swedish government in December 1940, the result was a vehicle similar to the L-62 that would be produced by Ganz under licence as the 40M Nimród.

Production began immediately, with up to 135 being produced between 1940 and 1943. The 40M Nimród was a real revolution in the world of armoured vehicles, as with its 40 mm open cannon (the 36M Bofors L/60), it was able to perform both anti-aircraft and anti-tank missions (in Germany, while the first 40M Nimród was being produced, only the Flakpanzer I Ausf.A armed with a 20 mm cannon was available).

Hungary's other request for this vehicle was that it be up to the speed of the Hungarian army's armoured vehicles, which it fulfilled perfectly, reaching a speed of 47-50 km/h with a range of 30 km.

A peculiarity of the cannon it carried was its high rate of fire, reaching 120 rounds per minute with a bullet exit velocity of 881 m/sec (even though the average armament load was 160 bullets).

During combat use, it proved that, despite its anti-aircraft design, it could be very effective against light and in some cases medium armour, penetrating 46 mm armour at 100 metres and 30 mm at 1000 metres. Against it, it was poorly armoured (28 mm in the roof and 13 mm in the vertical areas) and its open turret gave it a high silhouette.

As the conflict progressed and Soviet armoured vehicles improved, the 40M Nimród continued to demonstrate its power against enemy light vehicles, infantry or cavalry. Efforts were made to improve the firepower of the Nimród by equipping them with the 42M Kerngranate, which allowed the Nimród to fire 15 cm hollow-point explosive anti-tank grenades (the Nimród with the 42/aM stabilised high-explosive anti-tank grenade). This was a muzzle-loading weapon similar to the operation of a grenade fired from a rifle. This prototype was not continued.

Another attempt to improve the vehicle was to equip it with an 80 mm cannon, but this project did not go ahead. The Hungarian Ministry of Defence considered using the 29.M 80 mm anti-aircraft gun or the 18.M 80 mm field gun on the chassis of the Nimród to provide a powerful tank destroyer capable of doing considerable damage to any battleships the Soviets might deploy on the front line.

But while trying to 'fit' certain parts together, it was realised in September 1940 that both the speed of the anti-aircraft gun and its recoil were too high for the frame on which it was to be mounted to withstand them. This made it necessary to discard this option in favour of the field gun, which in itself had the limitation of not being able to be incorporated into a turret with 360° rotation, but rather inserted into the frame with a lateral deviation of about 30° to the right and another 30° to the left, as well as -10° and 30° vertically. It was proposed to be fitted with an armour of around 50mm and a semi-automatic loading system, but this increased the cost and the project was finally cancelled in February 1942.

Finally, it should be mentioned that the Nimród variant of the Nimród, which carried the 44M Buzogányvető rocket launcher, has already been covered in the section on the Toldi.

2) Lehel armoured personnel carrier

From the Nimród came a practical armoured transport vehicle called the Lehel. Its birth was motivated by a 1942 request from the Hungarian Ministry of Defence, which emphasised Hungary's need for such a vehicle given the impossibility of being supplied by Germany with the famous Sd.Kfz.251/1. In 1942, Ganz proposed an adaptation of the Nimród 40M, from which the roof would be removed and adapted to troop transport functions.

Two versions of the new vehicle were developed: the Lehel A (troop transport with a capacity of eight infantrymen and armed with a machine gun) and the Lehel S (medical transport with the capacity to carry four stretchers).

Although the complete project was presented in 1943, the war situation did not allow for such a brilliant project, which would have been very useful for the Magyar infantrymen.

▲ Due Turán II distrutti, ma ancora con le gonne laterali quasi intatte, vengono preparati per il trasferimento.

Comparative table of other armoured vehicles in service in Hungary:

	ORIGIN	CREW MEMBERS	WEIGHT (tonnes)	MAIN WEAPON	SPEED Km/h	MAIN BLINDNESS (mm)
Zrínyi II	HUNGARY		21.5	105 mm	40	75
Zrínyi I	HUNGARY		21.5	75 mm	40	75
Ansaldo	ITALY		6.8	8 mm	43	40
Csaba	HUNGARY		5.9	8 mm	65	
Nimrod	HUNGARY		10.9	40 mm	50	

OTHER FOREIGN-MADE ARMOURED VEHICLES

1) Tatra Koprivnice T-72 (OA vz.30)

The OA vz. 30, also known as the T-72, was a Czechoslovakian-made six-wheeled armoured vehicle, one example of which fell into the hands of Hungary in 1939.

2) Sd.Kfz.7 (Hansa-Lloyd HL m 10)

There are some photos showing the Hungarian use of some of these powerful half-tracks. The Hungarian army may also have had some Sd.Kfz.8s of larger tonnage than the Sd.Kfz.7s.

3) Sd.Kfz.11 (Hansa-Lloyd HL kl 5) / 37M

In 1937, Hungary purchased 74 examples of the 37M Hansa Lloyd tractor, better known by its German designation Sd.Kfz.11, from the German government. These were used as tractors for the Bofors 40 mm anti-aircraft guns and the 37M 105 mm light howitzers.

4) Sd.Kfz.251

This German vehicle in ambulance form, called Sd.Kfz.251/8, was also part of the Hungarian armoured fleet. It is known that at least the 2nd Armoured Division had one at the end of 1944, with the Red Cross emblem. Perhaps other Sd.Kfz.251s in a medical version were used by the Magyars from 1942 onwards.

ANNEX 2: HUNGARIAN ARMOURED TRAINS

In 1920, the Hungarian army had nine armoured trains, a remnant of the imperial era. In 1929, five of them were scrapped due to their deplorable condition, while four remained in service. In spite of this, the Hungarian military leadership considered these trains to be of great use due to their unbeatable ability to travel the length and breadth of the country, so they thought of improving both their passive and armament performance.

Thus, in 1938, these four trains, which were still in the Hungarian arsenal, were modified and equipped with 80 mm cannons as main armament. Between 1932-1934, these trains were armoured and refurbished and numbered as follows:
- 101: with one 80 mm cannon, one 37 mm cannon, two 20 mm anti-tank guns and six 8 mm machine guns.
- 102: as above.
- 103: as above.
- 104: one 80 mm cannon, one 20 mm anti-tank gun, two 8 mm machine guns.

These armoured trains were used independently of other units, participating in various actions.

In 1938, trains 101 and 102 participated in the recovery of northern Hungary.

In 1939, the four trains participated in the occupation of the Ukrainian Carpathians. In these actions, the trains were decorated because of their minimal resistance against the Hungarians.

In 1940, all trains participated in the occupation of Transylvania, although only train 102 entered the region.

In 1941, all trains participated in the actions against Yugoslavia.

During the campaign in the USSR, they could not be used due to the different track gauge between the two countries. However, they were able to use armoured trains, thanks to those captured by the Soviets in the Ukraine. The Eastern occupation group used a train against partisans in Bryantsk between 1942 and 1944, while the Western occupation group captured an old Polish train in Upper Hungary (which had been abandoned in 1944).

Trains 101 to 104 participated in the defence of Hungary. The 102nd supported the advance of the 2nd Army into Transylvania, capturing an important railway crossing at Marosbogát, beyond the Romanian lines, on 6 September 1944. This crossing, with its bridge, resisted without help until the troops of the 2nd Armoured Division arrived.

In late 1944 and early 1945, trains also participated in the fighting around Budapest and Lake Balaton. In Budapest, three armoured trains took part in the fighting, based at Keleti station. From their positions on the various railway branches, they were used as artillery points thanks to their 80 mm cannons.

ANNEX 4: NUMBER OF ARMOURED VEHICLES DEPLOYED BY THE HUNGARIANS

Below is an approximate number of the most important models of armoured vehicles used by the Hungarians during the years of the Second World War. Despite various studies on the subject, there is no unanimity on these figures, so we will stick to the most reliable data.

	1939	1940	1941	1942	1943	1944	1945	TOTAL
Panzer I				9				10 (1 in 1937)
R-35								
M 3 Stuart								
T-11								
Pcs 38				108				108
H-35/H-39								
S-35								
Pz III				10		10-12		20-22
Pz IV F1								
Pz IV F2				10				10
Pz IV H						+52	+20	+72
Pz V A						10-12		10-12
Pz VI						10-13		10-13
T-34/76-85			+10					+10
Toldi I-II-IIa	190			Various modifications: 80 types II become IIa				190
Turan I				279				279
Turan II					+180			+180
Marder II				5				5
StuG III						50-60		50-60
Hetzer						75-150		75-150
Csaba	145							145
Ansaldo								120-152 (in 1935-36)
Nimród			135					135
Zrínyi II					66-72			66-72

BIBLIOGRAPHY

Unknown, *The Royal Hungarian gendarmerie and police during world war II.*

Axworthy, Mark. *Third Axis Fourth Ally.* Arms and Armour. 1995.

Baczoni, Tamás; Tóth, László. *Hungarian Army Uniforms. 1939-1945.* Huniform Books. 2010.

Barnaky, Péter. *Panther on the battlefield.* Volume 6. PeKo Publishing. 2014.

Becze, Csaba. *Magyar Steel.* Stratus. 2006.

Bernád, Denes; Kliment, Charles K. *Magyar warriors. The history of the Royal Hungarian Armed Forces 1919-1945.* Volume I. Helion & Company. 2015.

Bernád, Denes; Kliment, Charles K. *Magyar warriors. The history of the Royal Hungarian Armed Forces 1919-1945.* Volume II. Helion & Company. 2017.

Bonhardt, Attila. *Zrínyi II assault howitzer.* PeKo Publishing. 2015.

Caballero, C; Molina, L. *Panzer IV. El puño de la Wehrmacht.* AF Editores. 2006.

Gladysiak, L; Karmieh, S. *Panzer IV Ausf. H and Ausf.J.* Vol I. Kagero 2015.

Gladysiak, L; Karmieh, S. *Panzer IV Ausf. H and Ausf.J.* Vol II. Kagero 2016.

Guillemot, Philippe. H*ungary 1944-45. The panzers' last stand.* Histoire&Collections. 2010.

Kerekes András. *The role and creation of the Royal Hungarian assault artillery, and the Zrínyi II assault howitzers.* Hadmérnök. X Évfolyam 2 szám. 2015 június.

Magyaródy, SJ. *Hungary and the Hungarians.* Matthias Corvinus Publishers.

Mc Taggart, Patrick. *¡Asedio!.* Inédita Editores SL. 2010.

Mujzer, Peter. *Huns on wheels.* Mujzer&Partner Ltd.

Oliver, Dennis. *Tiger I and Tiger II tanks.* Germany army and Waffen-SS Eastern Front 1944. Pen & Sword Military. 2016.

Order of battle and handbook of the Hungarian armed forces. February 1944. USA War department.

Restayn, Jean. *Tiger I in action 1942-1945.* Histoire & Collections.2013.

Thomas, Nigel; Pál Szábo, László. *The Royal Hungarian Army in World War II.* Osprey Publishing. 2008.

Tirone, Laurent. Panzer. *The German tanks encyclopedia.* Caraktere. 2016.

Ungváry, Krisztián. *Battle for Budapest.100 days in World War II.* IB Tauris. 2003.

Ungváry, Krisztián. *The "Second Stalingrad": The destruction of Axis forces at Budapest (february 1945).* Hungarian Studies Review, Vol XXII, nº 1 (Spring, 1995).

Wood, Ian Michael. *History of the Totenkopf´s Panther-Abteilung.* PeKo Publishing. 2015.

Zaloga, Steven J. *Tanks of Hitler´seastern allies. 1941-45.* Osprey Publishing. 2013.

TITOLI GIÀ PUBBLICATI - TITLES ALREADY PUBLISHING

BOOKS TO COLLECT

www.ingramcontent.com/pod-product-compliance
Lightning Source LLC
LaVergne TN
LVHW070522070526
838199LV00072B/6682